SEEKING
MINO-PIMATISIWIN

SEEKING MINO-PIMATISIWIN

An Aboriginal Approach to Helping

Michael Anthony Hart

Fernwood Publishing • Halifax

Chapter three revises and expands on previously published material.
Michael Hart, 2000. "An Aboriginal approach to social work practice." in T. Heinonen
    and L. Spearman (eds.), Problem Solving and Beyond: An Introduction to Social Work
    Practice. Toronto: Irwin Press.
Michael Hart, 1999. "Seeking minopimatasiwin: An Aboriginal approach to social work
    practice." Native Social Work Journal: Nishnaabe Kinoomaadwin Naadmaadwin 2(1).

Editing: Brenda Conroy
Cover art: Gerald Thickfoot
        The cover art was drawn by my late brother, Gerald Thickfoot. It is with my
        deep appreciation of his many gifts that it leads this work.
Design and production: Beverley Rach
Printed and bound in Canada by: Hignell Printing Limited

fifth reprint July 2007

A publication of Fernwood Publishing
Site 2A, Box 5, 32 Oceanvista Lane, Black Point, Nova Scotia, B0J 1B0
and 324 Clare Avenue, Winnipeg, Manitoba, R3L 1S3
www.fernwoodpublishing.ca

Fernwood Publishing Company Limited gratefully acknowledges the financial support
of the Department of Canadian Heritage, the Nova Scotia Department of Tourism and
Culture and the Canada Council for the Arts for our publishing program.

National Library of Canada Cataloguing in Publication Data

Hart, Michael, 1965-
    Seeking mino-pimatisiwin: an aboriginal approach to helping

Includes bibliographical references.
ISBN 978-1-55266-073-7

    1. Counseling. 2. Helping behavior. 3. Native peoples—Counseling of. 4. Social
work with native peoples. I. Title.

E98.S46H37 2002   362.2'04256   C2001-904138-1

TABLE OF CONTENTS

THIS IS DEDICATED TO MY GROWING CHILD. I WILL FOREVER LOVE YOU. MAY THE CREATOR WATCH OVER YOU AND YOUR MOTHER, WALK WITH YOU, AND GUIDE YOU THROUGHOUT YOUR LIFE.

ACKNOWLEDGEMENTS

First and foremost, I humbly offer my deepest love and gratefulness to our Creator. Nanaskomon Kici-manito. Nanaskomon Ma'mawi-o'hta'wima'w.

I am most deeply thankful to my family. My mother Vivian Thickfoot, you have instilled in me the faith in our Creator, the commitment to the well-being of people, the honour of our Cree people, the belief in one's abilities including my own, and the love for our family. May my life be a reflection of all this and demonstrate my gratefulness for what you have given me. My sister Fjola Hart-Wasekeesikaw, you are one of the greatest role models anyone could ask for. I am so grateful that you have looked out for me, guided me, and supported me as I wrote this book, and more importantly, throughout my life. Without you and Kim, my life certainly would have been a struggle beyond words. My niece Kimberly Wasekeesikaw Hart, I am blessed that you have showered me with love and gentleness which has reminded me to appreciate life and enjoy each day for what it presents. My brother Ronn Janes and my sister-in-law Fariel Janes, your continuous support and acceptance, no matter what is happening in life, have provided me with many joys and helped me through many struggles. My niece/godchild Jessica, your playfulness and humour shines on me so warmly and has provided so much for my growth as a human being. My godchildren, Jason, Donald and Jordan, by being in my life you have ensured my commitment to living a good life with the hope that all my efforts will come around to bless you. My extended family, whether we are close or far apart, you remain in my heart and prayers. My brothers, Gerald and Jimmy, while your journeys have taken you to another place, your lives and struggles are reflected in us, your family. I can only pray that how I live my life brings honour to you for what you have provided us. My grandparents—Grandma Hart, Grandpa Hart, Bush Grandpa and Grandma Thickfoot—I will forever carry and live out your love, wisdom and guidance as best I can. May my life honour yours.

While many Elders and cultural teachers have supported me directly and indirectly, there are some who have provided me with much direction and guidance at various periods in my life. Some of them include Marlene, Marie, Doris, Mariam, Veronique, Margaret, Dorothy, Isabel, Pearl, Marie Ann, Madeline, Noah, Lawrence, Walter, Wellington, William, William, Dominique, Harrison, Eddie and Peter. I am forever grateful. I pray that I live out and pass on your teachings in the most humble and respectful ways that they deserve.

As my immediate family is small, there have been many friends who have become my "family by choice." Beyond the Elders and teachers in my life, this family includes: Mervin and Sharon, Ed and Theresa, Leslie and Crystal, Hellen and Stuart, Winona and Billy, Jackie and Felix, Barb and Andy Daniels, Lionel and Lou, Bill and Martha, Mary and Carl, Lorne, Caroline, Barb, Ida, Stuart, Edna, Ann Marie, Keith, Tony, Winona, Amos, Bill, Brenda, Jill, Debbie, Adrienne, Bernice, Gordie, Tracy and Ken. Each of you and your families have provided me with joy, support and encouragement that have helped me strive towards being a better person. I can only hope that I am able to reflect these joys, support, encouragements, and in certain cases teasing words (you know who you are!) back to you.

To the citizens of Fisher River Cree Nation, whether our people live at home or far beyond, we share a common history and are forever tied through our ancestors. May you be blessed for the support you have provided me in my journey. To my past and present co-workers at Anishinaabe Mino-Ayaawin and the Faculty of Social Work, University of Manitoba, your support and encouragement have been a blessing to me. I am deeply grateful.

I also acknowledge the many people who have helped me bring these ideas to these pages. I believe that without the support, direction and positive persistent encouragement from Wayne Antony of Fernwood Publishing, this book would still be in its thesis state. I am deeply grateful to you Wayne. I am grateful to all the staff at Fernwood Publishing. In particular, I am thankful for the support and encouragement I received from Beverley Rach and Brenda Conroy. I am thankful for the reviewers who have provided suggestions and words of encouragement that helped me to further clarify my own ideas and thoughts. In particular, I offer a deep thank you to Fyre Jean Graveline, Director of the First Nations and Aboriginal Counselling Degree Program at Brandon University, and Jacquie Rice-Green, Professor at the Faculty of Social Work, University of Victoria.

There are certainly individuals that I unintentionally have left out. I may have misspelled someone's name. In either case, this is certainly only because of my weak mind and is not a reflection of the feelings in my heart for the dear people in my life.

I believe that we have been blessed in that our paths have crossed with one another. I pray that the blessing you have provided me will come full circle back to you. May the Creator be with each of you and your families throughout your journeys.

CHAPTER ONE

REMEMBERING WHERE I CAME FROM

Through my experience with Elders, traditional healers and Aboriginal helpers who have incorporated our values, beliefs and practices into their work, I have witnessed our own ways of helping. I have participated in ceremonies that have contributed to the healing and wellness of many people, both Aboriginal and non-Aboriginal. All of this has convinced me, as a social worker, that our ways of helping can be followed in social work and other helping practices. Unfortunately, this conviction is not shared throughout the helping fields.

Historically, the social work and psychology professions have acted as an extension of Amer-European[1] systems imposing colonial processes of oppression (Duran and Duran 1995; McKenzie 1985). In fields such as child welfare and mental health, Euro-centric helpers have pressured and coerced Aboriginal people to follow the ways of the societies that they established in the Americas. Most often this has meant assimilation and the internalization of colonial processes. I concur with the Canadian Association of Social Workers' (1994: 158) statement that the social work profession's ethnocentric practices and disrespect of Aboriginal cultures have produced anger, distrust and a lack of confidence among Aboriginal peoples towards the profession. Aboriginal people recognized long ago the need for fundamental changes to social work practices within Aboriginal cultures and have been calling for these changes for many years (see Mawhiney 1995; Morrissette, McKenzie and Morrissette 1993; Schwager, Mawhiney and Lewko 1991). In particular, they have strongly emphasized that traditional Aboriginal practices have to be acknowledged and supported as a method of healing for Aboriginal people (Absolon 1993; Clarkson et al. 1992; Hamilton and Sinclair 1991; Hodgson 1992; McCormick 1995; McKenzie and Morrissette 1993; Morrissette et al. 1993; Royal Commission on Aboriginal Peoples 1997).

As a Cree man who works in the field of social work I am committed to following our peoples' call for the use of Aboriginal ways of helping. This book is one of my attempts at fulfiling this commitment. It is born out of my work in a Master of Social Work program. It is based on writings about Aboriginal ways of helping, my discussions with Aboriginal helpers and my reflections upon my own participation in sharing circles. Most significantly, it incorporates my personal life experiences with helping. So, while it is based upon many ideas expressed by others, it remains my understanding of Aboriginal approaches to helping. This is not "the" approach representing all Aboriginal peoples. It is important to remember that within Canada there are more than fifty Aboriginal languages, over six hundred reserves, hundreds of Metis and Inuit communities, and thousands upon thousands of Aboriginal people living in towns and cities. To believe that there is one Aboriginal approach to helping would be naive, to say the least. When all the peoples are lumped together under the term Aboriginal, their various worldviews and practices are easily distorted. Unfortunately, there are many times when the terms Aboriginal, First Nations and Native are used out of convenience, and thus little attention is paid to particular groups of peoples, particularly by the dominating Amer-European societies. On the other hand, Aboriginal peoples face common challenges—colonial oppression being one of the greatest—which encourage the identification of commonalities among us. Thus, my intent in writing this book is to develop and present an approach to helping that will, I hope, stimulate our people to discuss and critique this and other Aboriginal approaches to helping. Key to these critiques will be the voices of individuals from particular nations identifying how this and other approaches support their worldviews in the helping processes. From these dialogues I hope that we will carry these approaches further, if not develop new, more effective ones.

What I Offer

This book is about an Aboriginal approach to helping. It addresses several topics, each of which relates to the others and all of which tend to support the need and/or application of this Aboriginal approach. In order to explain the need for an Aboriginal approach, I briefly discuss colonization from an Aboriginal perspective, ontological imperialism, social work's role in colonial oppression and the dynamic of resistance. I share an experience I had in order to demonstrate that ontological imperialism is still occurring today. I close this chapter by explaining the role this Aboriginal approach has in resisting these forms of colonial oppression. Chapter three outlines the foundational principles, values and views upon which Aboriginal helping methods are based. The Aboriginal approach outlined is general in nature in that it does not focus on specific issues. Further, since it relies broadly upon Aboriginal concepts, values and perspectives, it can be effectively incorporated by helpers trained in disciplines which involve counselling, supporting and teaching.

Chapter four discusses one specific Aboriginal helping method—sharing circles, chosen because they are already established within many Aboriginal cultures. Information that I relate about sharing circles is based upon a small body of writing about them and also on my reflective exploration of them. This involved talking intensely with five individuals who have conducted[2] sharing circles: Bernie, Fanny, Glen, Marg and Mary.[3]

Bernie, a Cree woman, has been a social worker for several years and has conducted sharing circles regularly, particularly in one of her positions serving women in a residential setting. She has also participated in sharing circles outside of her workplace. Fanny, a Cree woman, has worked as a nurse for many years. She has frequently conducted and participated in sharing circles, both within and outside her work experiences. Glen, a Cree man, has worked in social work positions and has explored the ways of many peoples. He has frequently participated in and conducted the sharing circle in personal and work settings. Marg, a Cree woman, has worked in various positions related to helping, the most recent being in a residential treatment program that regularly and frequently incorporates sharing circles. The eldest of the individuals interviewed, Marg, has learned about sharing circles and other Cree practices for many years. She has recently begun teaching about these practices to others who approach her with a request to learn. Mary, a Cree woman, has worked as a social worker and traditional counsellor in various settings, including a residential treatment centre and a shelter for families facing abusive situations. She has been conducting and participating in sharing circles for years both within her work and in her personal life. While all five have participated in ceremonial practices beyond sharing circles, four of them consistently and regularly participate in and/or conduct ceremonies. While all of them presently reside in Aboriginal communities, they each have had the experience of residing in communities where Aboriginal people are not the majority of the population. In the fourth chapter I also draw together the written material on sharing circles and this Aboriginal approach and highlight the commonalities between this approach and sharing circles. Sharing circles are used to represent important aspects of Aboriginal cultures, since they have been used and continue to be used by Aboriginal peoples in helping situations. In Chapter Five, I discuss how the Aboriginal approach is and can be used in various situations including work with individuals, families and groups. I also describe how the approach is followed when addressing family violence. I close the chapter with an example of the Aboriginal approach and sharing circles being used together with a focus on building the self-esteem of youth.

Where My Heart Lies

I remember the words of a dear friend who has been actively learning about our Cree ways for many, many years. She had cautioned a mutual friend that we have to be careful when we read books to try to learn about our ways because we never get to know the authors; we don't know what they are like or where their hearts lie. With her words echoing in my mind, I was concerned that readers would not know where I was coming from and, in turn, not know the background to the information in this book. While I cannot truly share myself with you in ways that you would come to know me as a human being, I offer these few words as a step towards understanding where my heart lies.

I am a Cree man. I am a citizen of Fisher River Cree Nation but I reside in Winnipeg, Manitoba. While I frequently travelled the two hundred plus kilometres north to Fisher River and Dallas, Manitoba, to visit my grandparents as a child, I was raised in Winnipeg by my mother, Vivian Thickfoot. My family consists of my mother and niece, Kim, who both reside in Winnipeg, my sister Fjola (Fj sounds like that in fjord), who now makes her home in Norway House, Manitoba, my little grandma Edith (little being a term of endearment), who lives in Peguis, and my traditionally adopted brother Ronn, his wife Fariel and my niece Jessica. At one hundred years of age, my grandma is older than her weight in pounds! Besides my other grandparents, my two brothers have travelled to the other side. My oldest brother, Jimmie, passed away when I was a baby, and my second brother, Gerald, passed away in 1992. I have many aunties, uncles and cousins spread from Fisher River, Little Saskatchewan and Norway House, Manitoba, to Toronto and Ottawa, Ontario. Some are close to me, others are getting closer, and some I haven't met … yet. I am also blessed with a "family of choice" made up of very close Elders and friends.

Among the first Cree families to live in Winnipeg, my mother faced many challenges raising four children on her own, including poverty, isolation and racism. Apparently, the Children's Aid Society came to the hospital very soon after my birth to take me away. The social worker said it was because my mother was single and already had three children. This was the time of the "sixties scoop"[4] and a time when single parents were not looked upon well. Fortunately, my mother was, and is, a strong woman. She fought off the social worker and pulled in support, a church minister, who came and stood by her. Others weren't so lucky. My mothers recalls that there were several other Native women on the same hospital floor at that time who, soon after delivery, lost their babies to the Children's Aid

Society. She tells one story that ends with her watching a friend stand in the street sobbing while her friend's last child is driven away by a social worker. Even when the Children's Aid came regularly to the door for the six months following my birth, my mother hid us in the closet and called the minister to get rid of them. She always fought to keep us together as a family, no matter what we faced.

One of the most significant choices my mother made when I was a child, and which has affected my life greatly to this day, regards our language. While I grew up listening to my mom speaking Cree to my grandparents, aunties and uncles, as well as her friends and co-workers, I did not grow up hearing her speak Cree to me or my siblings. When I was an adult and before my mother lost her ability to speak—due to a burst aneurysm and stroke—she was teaching me Cree. It was during one our "lessons" that she explained how much she and others were put down for speaking Cree. One story was about her witnessing a teacher put a clothespin on a fellow student's tongue for speaking Cree. She also believed that the best start she could give us in life was to teach us English. Besides, she would say, "you kids never wanted to learn."

Despite all the challenges of our life, I have many fond memories. When I was a child we lived in the core area and later the north end of Winnipeg. I remember playing at the Native Club and getting hamburgers from my auntie who worked there, going to pow wows to watch my older sister dance, playing street hockey with my brother and watching television at my auntie's home in Point Douglas while my mother and her visited over bannock, lard and tea. We later moved to low rental housing located in River Heights/Tuxedo, a very wealthy area of Winnipeg. All the stories related to low income kids surrounded by kids from PMQs (personal military quarters) and affluent families are too numerous to mention here.

Around the time of this move, my mother got a job working with the Native Alcoholism Council of Manitoba. The first time I can really recall Elders visiting our family is associated with her work there. My mom spent much time learning from Elders. She never forced us, her children, to follow her in her learning. Because of her experiences as a child, she had made a decision long before to let us determine our own path. Despite this choice, we still had opportunities to spend time with these Elders and had indirect moments of listening as they talked with my mom. Other moments were more direct. I remember sitting in a sharing circle in a church basement as a young boy. There must have been at least forty people there, with two Elders conducting the circle. While I didn't understand all that was happening, since much of the conversation was in Cree, I sure felt it. The feeling from that ceremony never left me, and I am thankful for the experience and the time with those two old men.

When I was twelve, two things happened to my immediate family which affected us as greatly as any event we ever faced. One was the birth of my niece. She brought a new commitment to our family. I think her birth encouraged my sister, who already had her diploma in nursing, to go back to school to obtain a degree. She later graduated with a Bachelor of Nursing degree in 1982. Along with my mother's constant encouragement for us to go to school since "it's a way out," my sister's lead in this area influenced our family more than I can explain. The second thing to happen was my brother Gerald, at the age of eighteen, being diagnosed with rheumatoid arthritis. From just prior to that point to the end of his life, my brother lived in constant pain. There were many times in the middle of the night when I watched my mother cradle him in her arms as he cried. Later, he stopped the sobbing. In one of his stays in the hospital, he would listen to people older than him complain about and compare their pain, and he didn't want to grow up doing that. He explained to me that this was his reality and he was going to live with it. To him, this meant going to university and getting an education. He graduated with a Bachelor of Social Work degree in 1986, after many years of alternating school with hospital stays. I believe if I have any strength or compassion in my heart, I gained it from my family.

My formative years in grade school were bittersweet. While I made many wonderful friends from all sort of backgrounds, I also learned about stereotypes and racism and my anger. All too often, I let out this in anger in self-destructive ways. I am thankful that despite these challenges I was able to enter university in 1984 through the University of Manitoba Special Premedical Studies Program (SPSP). If it wasn't for this program I would not have been eligible to attend university because of to my poor grades in high school. SPSP focused upon my abilities and potential, not my limits. It is an access program providing support to individuals who face social, educational, cultural and economic barriers. At that time it provided personal counsellors and extra academic and financial supports to individuals wanting to enter a health profession. I wanted to become a physician, specifically a psychiatrist. However, after two and half years of preparing to enter the Faculty of Medicine, I changed my mind and decided that social work's wider perspective would fit more with my views. After another two and half years I graduated from the Bachelor of Social Work program in 1989. One of the things I learned through my experiences was that, given the opportunity, support and desire, anyone can reach goals they thought were impossible.

Four days after my graduation I began my first job, as a case manager for Winnipeg Centre Child and Family Services. Based in the core area of Winnipeg, I was blessed with the opportunity to work with many families, most of whom were Aboriginal. The people were always teaching me something, usually something about myself. I was always amazed at their resilience. Despite the amazing odds they faced, they managed to survive one way or another. Some of my co-workers would get upset when they were scammed out of bus tickets or parcels of food, but I thought it was right on that the families we served had learned enough about the system to manipulate it and get what they needed as they understood it. I was also reminded how oppressive social workers can be. I remember two workers who would speak about being the best mothers around and how they would save these poor children; usually this meant apprehension. Indeed, they had among the highest apprehension rates around. I never believed that the best way to help a family was by tearing it apart. If I had to apprehend, it was the toughest thing I did. I remember one large family that I was working to try to keep together. The file about them had been open for years, and it seemed that they were written off as a family. While I worked with this family, they remained together one way or another. The mother always had contact with her children and provided direction on how things should be handled. Once I left the agency, this family was dismantled to the point that the mother did not know where her children were. Her biggest crime was that she couldn't control her children's actions. I truly disbelieve that foster parents or a levelling system of care could do better than her. The true difference was that foster parents and the care system had far more resources, albeit limited, than this mother. On the other hand, I also recall how abusive some parents could be to children, and I knew that these children needed safe homes. To me safe homes meant aunties, uncles and grandparents, not strangers. Among the many things I learned from this first working experience was that our people have very different perspectives and realities than Amer-Europeans, regardless of whether we are receiving services from them or working alongside them. Often these differences, not ourselves, determine the fate of our people.

Soon after my experience in child welfare, I moved to Whitehorse, Yukon, and started working on a Master of Social Work degree by taking my electives through correspondence. It wasn't too long after my move that I found myself in a term position with the Council for Yukon Indians, as the Yukon Native Alcohol and Drug Addictions Program treatment manager. I was hired to implement a new service program developed by a consultant and a committee of individuals from the communities. However, when it came time for me to implement the program, none of the communities were aware of the predetermined direction of the program and it was halted. As a result, I ended up reviewing and analyzing services being implemented by the federal and territory governments and their impact on the First Nations peoples in Yukon. Throughout this experience I was learning how important self-determination is to Aboriginal peoples, on both the community and nation level.

During this time in Yukon, I had become very close to a Tlingit family, so close, in fact, that one member presented to me the idea of adopting me into the family, thus the clan. If you understand the beauty of Yukon, you would know the significance of this idea. Upon being informed of the idea, one Elder, a beautifully wise woman I had become close to spoke with me. She talked about the clan system and what it would mean to be adopted into one. She discussed what being Tlingit meant to her and the commitment that would be expected of me. She discussed my connection to the Cree people and territory. Through her words I was learning, on a different, more intense level, about the importance of my identity and my connection to the land and people.

I returned to Winnipeg not only to complete my degree but to continue my learning about Cree values, beliefs and practices that I had actively started before I moved to Yukon. That fall, my brother Gerald passed away. This had a tremendous effect on me in more ways than one would expect. I reflected upon his zest for life, regardless of the barriers he faced. I recalled my mother's words about how short life is and recognized my desire to live life fully. My brother was working on his Master of Social Work degree and teaching for the Faculty of Social Work at Thompson at the time of his passing. A memorial was held in his honour in Thompson and I was asked to attend. It was then that I got to know the people at the faculty site. Later that spring I was asked to teach a course over the summer. Before the completion of the course, I was offered a one-year contract to teach at the site, and that one year ended up being five years.

The program was an access program, just like the one that helped me through my first degree. To come full circle and teach within such a program was a true blessing for me. More so was the learning the students offered to me. These students had left their homes throughout northern Manitoba to attend the program in Thompson. Most of them were Aboriginal women with families. While not everyone who enrolled completed the program, the graduation rate has been, for the most part, greater than that of the university in general. Considering that the program's content included material taught on the main campus in Winnipeg and additional material to support the program's appropriateness for a northern setting, I believe the students have more than demonstrated their resilience and abilities. Their consistent questioning of the appropriateness of what they were learning and their commitment to their families, communities and people, along with my own critique of the content of the various course, challenged me to find material and examples which were inclusive of Aboriginal peoples' experiences. I was also spending significant time with Cree Elders and ceremonial leaders while I was in Thompson, as well as travelling across the prairies to learn from various Cree people. In fact, I became so consumed in the teaching and learning that it took me a total of six years to complete the Master of Social Work degree. It was through the teachings from these people, the students' desires for relevant curriculum, the completion of my thesis on an Aboriginal approach and my commitment to the well-being of Aboriginal peoples, that I recognized the need for our views to be included in the social work curriculum.

I then returned to Winnipeg to prepare for my next dream, my doctorate degree. I began working with Health Canada's Medical Services Branch (now referred to as First Nations and Inuit Health Branch) through an interchange agreement with Anishinaabe Mino-Ayaawin (AMA), which is a First Nations health organization serving seven First Nations in the Interlake region of Manitoba. I lasted three and half months with Health Canada before I realized I couldn't work on that side of the fence. I have since been working directly for AMA, as a manager setting up their mental health program. My experiences here show me the limitless abilities of Aboriginal people when given the opportunity to develop, implement and deliver programs that follow the direction and desires of the people we serve.

These experiences have shaped me, particularly in my role as a social worker, and I have come to hold certain beliefs very strongly. I believe all people have abilities, some of which are more pronounced than others. Many Aboriginal peoples refer to these as gifts. I believe we are to seek out these gifts and try to understand how they are to be used. Indeed, this belief is demonstrated in our peoples practices of fasts, vision quests and the deep contemplation experienced in many ceremonies. I believe we are to use our gifts for the betterment, wellness and self-determination, not only of ourselves, but also of our families, communities and nations. I also believe that the differences between Aboriginal peoples' and non-Aboriginal peoples' worldviews, values, beliefs and practices are real. These differences challenge helping relationships between Aboriginal and non-Aboriginal peoples since the ability to make strong connections can be difficult as a result. I believe one of the best ways to help our own peoples is to use our abilities in a manner which follows and supports our peoples' perspectives, values, beliefs and practices. When differences arise between our own and other peoples' ways, then the most appropriate resolutions for us remain within the cultures of our peoples. I believe that our Elders, particularly those following our traditional ways, hold the deepest understanding of our cultures. As such, I believe our Elders hold many answers to how we are to resolve differences and concerns and the ability to set direction for Aboriginal peoples. Because of my experiences and beliefs, I have attempted to rely upon the wisdom of Elders.

FOLLOWING THE ELDERS' EXAMPLE

Of great significance to me and a great influence on my writing of this book are the many opportunities I had to spend time with Elders and in ceremonies. As a child I was greatly influenced by my grandparents. I hold many stories, memories and teachings from all of them. I recall one grandfather's love of the bush, sleeping under his Hudson Bay blankets, and listening to him hum as I fell asleep in his one-room house. I recall staying with my grandparents in Fisher River, listening to my grandfather as he prayed in Cree and listening to my grandmother as she told stories on how to behave and treat others. As a boy I was able to sit and listen to Elders as they visited with my mother or when they shared in circles. Later, I started attending ceremonies and took an active interest in learning about them. Before I left for Yukon, I began learning about Cree ceremonies and when I returned this work intensified.

One of the results of this interest and work is that I have followed our practices as I sought information for this book. I initiated the process which led to this book with a ceremony. Throughout my learning and writing I followed my grandfathers' examples by including prayer and song to help me. I remembered my grandmothers' commitment to helping others and attempted to maintain this commitment. As best I could, I followed the teachings Elders shared with me during our visits. For example, I incorporated the offering of tobacco. Tobacco has been used by Aboriginal people for centuries as part of an exchange between two or more people, animals, spirits and/or the Creator. Usually one individual will offer tobacco when requesting or appreciating something. When requests are made, the individual who is offered the tobacco is free not to accept it, thereby indicating that he or she is not prepared for various reasons to meet the request. The inclusion of tobacco emphasizes that the exchange will be, among many things, honest, respectful and kind. This inclusion of tobacco coincides with mainstream ethical concepts such as confidentiality and the rights of individuals to participate or not. In order to maintain a respectful and balanced relationship with the people I talked with, I offered tobacco to each of them when I made my request for information on sharing circles. When we were finished, I offered each of them a blanket in exchange for the gifts that they shared with me. In this way, I tried to follow the example the Elders had set.

I share these experiences and beliefs with you in order that I do not misrepresent myself and you can understand where I stand. I do not profess any great wisdom. More accurately, I am blessed in that through talking with Elders and many other Aboriginal people, I have obtained a little bit of an understanding of our people, of our ways of helping and of our aspirations. I am trying to further this understanding by using it as a guide for my daily life and in my helping practice with Aboriginal peoples. This learning and my beliefs are incorporated into these pages, but I must emphasize that I certainly do not think that my life and understanding is any better—or any worse—than what others have experienced and understand. Indeed, a phrase comes to mind when I think about sharing my perspective on helping: "I don't know anything."

"I Don't Know Anything"

I have heard this statement from many Elders, and I am still trying to come to grips with its meaning. I do realize that what I know is far from what these wise, old people know. To me, having information and knowing something are very different. I've been in school for most of my life in one form or another and I have been given a lot of information to hold. From my life experiences and reflections on these experiences I have come to know a little about myself. But when it comes to life and when I remember what these Elders have said, I get the sense that I really don't know much about anything out there. So when I pull together the ideas of many people, include my thoughts and offer these words about an Aboriginal approach to social work and other helping practices, it is within this context. I leave it up to you to decide what information you can come to know. Feel free to leave the rest.

NOTES

1. The term Amer-European as opposed to Euro-American, is used to empha-size the European base of people and their ideas.

2. Some people use alternative terms for conduct, specifically facilitate or host. Similarly, the word conductor, facilitator and host are used interchangeably. In following my experiences in northern Manitoba, I will primarily use the term conductor.

3. To ensure the anonymity of these sharing circle conductors, I am using pseudonyms for them. Indeed, two of the individuals interviewed preferred to remain anonymous.

4. The sixties scoop refers to the wave of apprehensions of Aboriginal children. Literally thousands of children were taken from their homes and adopted to non-Aboriginal families throughout Canada, the United States and Europe. While the name focuses on the sixties, this process of adopting out Aboriginal children continued right up to the middle of the 1980s. For further discussions on this matter, see Johnson (1983), McKenzie and Hudson (1985), and Fournier and Crey (1997).

CHAPTER TWO

EUROCENTRICISM, COLONIZATION AND RESISTANCE

I was having lunch with a new acquaintance who had recently started a position as a professor in a social work faculty. She was teaching a graduate course addressing clinical social work and, wanting to include an Aboriginal perspective, she had asked me to present on the topic to the class. From our first meetings to arrange this presentation I had become aware of her desire to learn more about Aboriginal people, the issues we face and our perspectives on how to address these issues. During our lunch we were discussing my interest in completing a doctoral degree, and she was sharing her experiences of women being treated oppressively in some of these programs. She highlighted these experiences to raise awareness of what I may experience as a Cree man.

We also continued our previous discussion of the issues Aboriginal people face, including colonization, oppression and social work's role in these destructive processes. I explained how I tried to incorporate these topics in every course I taught when I was working as professor in a program in which the majority of the students were Aboriginal and explained my perspective that social work education needs to address these issues not only as a distant, theoretical concern occurring in Aboriginal communities but also as they exist in universities, classrooms and curricula. She was aware of and in agreement to these points, and I identified several authors, such as Vine Deloria Jr. and Patricia Monture-Angus, who have and are addressing these issues. I said that Aboriginal people have their own theories, approaches and practices of helping, and I began outlining to her the explanations of Cree Elder Eddie Belrose of how Aboriginal people see the relationship between individuals, families, communities and nations. I began drawing the diagram of four circles, one inside each other, that I had seen in various books. In the centre circle I wrote the word "individual" and put in brackets the word "me" beside it. In the next surrounding circle, I wrote the word "family." In the third circle I wrote the word "community." As I was writing the word "nation" in the final outer circle, she interrupted with, "Oh, the ecological approach."

My heart sank. I realized that, despite our several conversations and my presentation in her class, she was still maintaining the Amer-European view of society. She was not able to see, nor would she take the time to see, this diagram for what it was, a teaching from one of our Elders. My disappointment was compounded by the fact that the first time this teaching had been shared with me was in the early to mid-seventies, when I was a boy. During his many visits to my family, Eddie had taught my mother, and me indirectly, about our people's holistic understanding of the universe and how people related to one another. He had also explained that he'd been taught this a long time before by an old man he referred to as "grandfather."

From my experiences with Eddie and many other Elders, it is clear to me that our teachings have existed for a time longer than I can imagine. So, when someone who is responsible for teaching upcoming social workers about Aboriginal helping perspectives, theories and practices interprets one of our basic long standing teachings as the ecological approach, a new-born Amer-European perspective, I am disheartened and left wondering what it will take in order for our ways to be respected as our ways.

Like so many other Aboriginal people who do not want to jump to conclusions about cultural expropriation, I shook off these thoughts and considered this to be an isolated incident. Regretfully, I went through a similar experience with another professor who had included cross-cultural studies as part of her focus. During an informal meeting, I opened a book on Native womanhood by Kim Anderson to show this professor a diagram which was an adaptation of the one explained by Eddie Belrose. This diagram had concentric circles with the words "individual," "family," and "community/nation" written in the first three circles. The final circle encompassed all the others and had the word "creation" written in it. Upon seeing this diagram, the second professor also called it the ecological approach. Again, the professor could not see it for what it was, even though she knew she was seeing a book on reconstructing Native woman-hood. Again, I was disheartened. Once again I was faced with a reflection of the colonial processes that our people have been facing for generations … and I hated it.

COLONIZATION FROM AN ABORIGINAL PERSPECTIVE

Aboriginal nations were once independent nations whose people relied upon and utilized the land in all aspects of our lives. Colonization is driven by a worldview that embraces dominion, self-righteousness and greed. These ideas affect all aspects of the relationship between the colonizers and the colonized—the Aboriginal peoples. The effects occur on all levels—nation, community, family, and individual.

On a national level, Aboriginal peoples were once autonomous and self-determining economically, politically, culturally and socially. Colonization involved the destruction of Aboriginal peoples' economic systems through the introduction of a foreign hierarchal system of economics that is based upon greed. With the imposition of this system, the colonizers develop and maintain the upper echelons of the system and use the profits gained to reaffirm this position for their own benefit. Through this process, colonizers develop the initial power over the colonized people. With this upper hand, the colonizers are able to manipulate and direct Aboriginal peoples' political processes. This is achieved by the colonizers recognizing only the leaders they prefer and offering agreements, such as treaties, where the well-being of the Aboriginal people is promised in exchange for access to the land. The leaders preferred are those ones who at least do not contradict the colonizers, and at best, actively support the systems established by the colonizers.

As the economic and political control over the people forms and increases, the colonizers introduce their worldviews to oppress Aboriginal peoples' cultures and act to destroy Aboriginal social institutions. The colonizers' desire to oppress Aboriginal cultures is based primarily upon two things. First, they hold a self-righteous stance that their views and actions are the proper and best ones to be held by all peoples of the world. In turn, Aboriginal peoples' worldviews are trivialized, our histories are rewritten from the eyes of the colonizers, and our values are demeaned and manipulated. The second reason lies with the colonizers' need to legitimize their dominion over Aboriginal peoples' land. If the Aboriginal peoples' cultures keep them tied to the land, then this connection needs to be severed so that the colonizers' claim over the land and its resources can be confirmed.

To make such a separation requires control over the peoples' cultures. Overt expressions of Aboriginal cultures, such as spiritual and recreational institutions, are desecrated and degraded. Aboriginal spiritual ceremonies are labelled as devil worshipping. Aboriginal gatherings and activities, such as feasts, give-aways, singing and dancing, are deemed sinful and are stopped when witnessed by agents or religious leaders of the colonizers. The peoples' connection to the land is considered an expression of our primitiveness. This cultural oppression is coupled with action that destroys Aboriginal peoples' social systems, such as our education, health and judicial institutions. Aboriginal methods of education, such as cooperative learning, are ignored or seen as inferior and are replaced by industrial and residential schools. Aboriginal peoples' ways to wellness and use of herbal remedies are deemed to be witchcraft and therefore evil. Our systems of justice, including teaching alternative or restorative behaviours, are considered ineffective. In these processes of oppressing the cultures and destroying the social institutions, along with economic and political exploitation, the colonizers continue and further develop their dominion, legitimize their self-righteousness, and establish and maintain greed.

These processes also tear apart Aboriginal communities and families. The people are forced to follow the leaders defined by the colonizers in order to access the promises made by the colonizers in their agreements.[1] The people are also required to reside on particular tracts of land—reserves or settlements—with other families with whom they may or may not have aligned themselves otherwise. While the agreements to establish these communities promise support for the livelihood and well-being of the people, the reality is that they serve to move Aboriginal people off the land desired by the colonizers. These newly made communities are ultimately governed by agents of the colonizers who, with the support of the colonizers' army and police force, are able to control and restrict the mobility of the people. This method of divide and conquer, along with laws which make particular gatherings illegal, also serve to limit the peoples' ability to organize politically.

Families are directly attacked by the colonizers and are forced to fit the colonizers' expectations and belief systems. At one point, Aboriginal families were well defined by extended family relationships which crossed generations and bloodlines. These relationships established intricate balances between the genders, generations and assigned responsibilities, and were the weave of Aboriginal communities. These relationships are torn apart and replaced by imposed structures which mimic the colonizers hierarchy and ideas of dominion, self-righteousness and greed. Our children are removed from our families and re-educated in the colonizers institutions, while the colonizers' agents attack Aboriginal family beliefs and structures through propaganda and manipulative force, such as withholding food rations. Disparities in the family are created where men are supported and encouraged to rule the home through the oppression of women and children. Our peoples' spirituality, which includes respecting all life, the importance of both genders and the sacredness of children, is oppressed by the colonizers' religions, which degrade views different from their own by labelling them as primitive and evil.

Colonization attacks individuals on the emotional, physical, mental and spiritual levels. Aboriginal persons are seen as savages, incapable of living up to the virtues of the colonizers. On the emotional level, colonizers consider Aboriginal people as unreasonably angry, depressed and ungrateful, since they are unable to appreciate the benefits bestowed upon them by the colonizers. Indeed, the colonizers demonstrate their self-righteousness through their belief that they have freely handed Aboriginal people benefits such as homes, schools and health systems and by remaining ignorant of the broken promises and the price paid by our people through the land, resources and lives. The colonizers contemptuously ridicule Aboriginal peoples' physical appearance, referring to it as dark, ugly and dirty. The view that we are dangerous is confirmed by the colonizers' erroneous rationalization processes. For example, the eugenics movement, where hereditary and physical characteristics were thought to determine a person's abilities socially, was used to justify the oppression of people who were different than the colonizer. Thus, the colonizer feels, at best, sympathy—"poor Indian"—or worse, contempt—"get out of my face, you've caused your own problems." On a spiritual level, Aboriginal people are torn by the contradiction imposed upon us by the colonizer. We are told that to be accepted by God, we must give up all that defines us as Aboriginal people. Yet, we are constantly reminded through ridicule that we can never give up the colour of our skin, hair or eyes; nor can we give up our heritage. In terms of our mental capacity, we are thought of as incompetent, unreasonable and incapable of learning the colonizers' ways when we speak out for our ideas. The knowledge held by Aboriginal people is not recognized until it is presented as new knowledge created by the colonizers.

Once Aboriginal persons internalize the colonization processes, we feel confused and powerless since we are pressured to detach from who we are and are left with no means to alleviate the pressure. We may implode with overwhelming feelings of sadness or explode with feelings of anger. Some try to escape this state through alcohol, drugs and/or other forms of self-abuse. We may ignore our health, ridiculing our traditional diet and eat only junk food that is made easily accessible by the colonizer. Thoughts of suicide even flow through us as a means out of the confusion and impoverishment. Aboriginal people start to believe that we are incapable of learning and that the colonizers' degrading images and beliefs about Aboriginal people and our ways of being are true. Following such beliefs, we too call down Aboriginal peoples and ways without taking the time to reflect on the colonization processes and who these beliefs serve. Aboriginal people try to follow the colonizers' religions and condemn anyone who reflects any aspect of Aboriginal ways.

Aboriginal families who have internalized the colonization processes and adapted to the hierarchal system are shells of violence, objectification and isolation. Relationships between emotionally isolated individuals are based upon their attempts to attain the lost sense of belonging and love. Yet, there is little giving without the expectation that something will be given in return. The more powerful family members seek physical gratification through sexual exploitation, a sense of worth that is based upon the degradation of other members, and slave-like services through threats and abuse. Thus, incidences of women being beaten by men, children being emotionally, physically and sexually abused by older family members, and men facing isolation become frequent as all family members are confronted daily with the pains of colonization. Individuals who try to overcome this pain through maintaining their sense of identity as Aboriginal persons and/or who attempt to educate themselves are scorned by other family and community members who have internalized the colonization process. Our communities remain divided since there is little support for one another to move ahead.

The internally colonized nations are torn apart as well since there is little unity. Leaders, following the examples of self-righteousness and greed demonstrated by the colonizer, rule by self-interest first and foremost. Power is used over the people, especially members of other families. Economic gains are also based upon self-interest. Those interested in establishing laws and governing forces which address these abuses are quickly disempowered—through covert force, such as stopping individuals and their families from accessing the limited resources available, or overt force, such as threats and violence. Other individuals would rather be governed and ruled by the colonizers and look to them for answers.

As Aboriginal people move further into internalizing the colonization processes, the more we degrade who we are as Aboriginal people. All of these internalized processes only serve the colonizers, who then are able to sit back and say "see, we were right." In colonizers' eyes, the usurpation is justified.

Ontological Imperialism—Social Work and Other Helping Professions

Battiste and Henderson (2000: 86) suggest that "the military, political, and economic subjugation of Indigenous peoples has been well documented, as have social, cultural, and linguistic pressures and the ensuing damage to Indigenous communities, but no force has been more effective in oppressing Indigenous knowledge and heritage than the education system." Amer-

European thinkers, including social work scholars, have maintained their tradition of creating knowledge. Their system is based upon breaking ecologies down into the smallest ideas, objects and/or events possible, so that each part can be classified and defined. As such, it requires precise measurement, prediction and control. Battiste and Henderson (2000) highlight that at no point does this system portray the "real" world more accurately than another does. The Amer-European system, with its ideas of universality and diffusion, assumes its superiority and attempts to impose its worldviews on the whole world. This diffusion and imposition of its worldviews serves a purpose, as explained by Linda Tuhiwai Smith (1999: 63): "The globalization of knowledge and Western culture constantly reaffirms the west's view of itself as the centre of legitimate knowledge, the arbiter of what counts as knowledge and the source of 'civilized' knowledge."

The Amer-Eurocentric view of and system for understanding reality ignores the diversity of Aboriginal peoples and our own views and systems. Aboriginal persons attempting to learn in these systems face a most oppressive situation:

> For most Indigenous students in Eurocentric education, realizing their invisibility is like looking into a still lake and not seeing their reflections. They become alien in their own eyes, unable to recognize themselves in the reflections and shadows of the world. In the same way Eurocentric thought stripped their grandparents and parents of their wealth and dignity, this realization strips modern Indigenous students of their heritage and identity. (Battiste and Henderson 2000: 88)

The Amer-European colonizers believe they have really contributed something to the well-being of Indigenous people. Memmi (1991: 75) explains that as the self-appointed custodians of the values of civilization and history, the colonizers believe they have accomplished a mission: "They have the immense merit of bringing light to the colonized's ignominious darkness. The fact that this role brings [them] privileges and respect is only justice; colonization is legitimate in every sense and with all its consequences." In other words, the colonizer has no idea about the reality of the oppressed. It is not incorporated as part of any curriculum; nor is it truly recognized as part of Aboriginal students' experiences. Battiste and Henderson identify this destructive process as ontological and cognitive imperialism and assert that "survival for Indigenous peoples is more than a question of physical existence; it is an issue of preserving Indigenous knowledge systems in the face of cognitive imperialism" (2000: 12).

Social work and other helping professions are not immune from these dynamics. These professions follow theories and approaches—from psychoanalysis to ecological and beyond—that are solely based in the realities of Amer-Europeans. While these professions espouse altruistic intentions, the reality is that they are not meant to challenge the colonial system. As Gil (1998: 14) explains, "an important function of social work and social services throughout history has been to modify and fine-tune the intensity of oppression and injustice in societies, and to ameliorate their destructive consequences for human development. Social work and social services were, however, never meant to eliminate inequalities, oppression and injustice, and their consequences." Indeed, the helpers in Amer-European systems are well trained to indirectly support the system, not overhaul it. Gil explains further:

> Social workers and social policy professionals have always been involved with victims of injustice and oppression. Yet, though they tend to grasp intuitively and emotionally the meaning of these dehumanizing conditions, they usually lack theoretical insights into their causes, and into strategies to transform unjust and oppressive social, economic, and political institutions into just and nonoppressive alternatives. (1998: 1)

More concerning is that through their misguided altruism, Amer-European scholars and practitioners oppress Aboriginal helping knowledge and practices. "Researchers and practitioners using western methodologies fail to realize how incompletely their methods capture the truth of Native American tribal lives and pathology. Western methods infiltrate Native American life worlds as epistemic violence, replacing Native American with foreign idioms, definitions, and understandings" (Duran and Duran 1995: 69). Aboriginal peoples seek to develop their own understanding of history and the relationship between issues of colonization, oppression and injustice and their links to such experiences as poverty, suicide, violence and ontological imperialism. Amer-Europeans reinterpret these understandings through an ahistorical, reductionistic stance; they break the issues down to an individual's problem and ignore the historical roots of the concerns. They fragment the issues into discrete parts that are based upon symptoms, rather than causes, such as racism, anti-Semitism, sexism and other discriminatory practices. The parts are then addressed without consideration to any of the similarities and relationships between the parts (Gil 1998).

As Duran and Duran (1995: 6) suggest, if the helping professions respected Aboriginal perspectives, they would incorporate processes and methodologies which directly address the effects of genocide, colonization and oppression. Instead, "the effects of the genocide are quite personalized and pathologized," as evidenced by the helping professions' use of diagnostic, assessment and labelling tools. For example, while an individual's feeling of hopelessness and/or rage may be noted through initial counselling processes, it is trivially referenced, if at all, to the multi-generational effect of colonial trauma and the larger socio-political realities. On the occasions when Aboriginal peoples' understandings are seen as having merit, and although cognitive imperialism devalues Indigenous knowledge and heritage, the dominant society members will take those desired elements of Indigenous knowledge out of context and claim them for themselves (Battiste and Henderson 2000).

RESISTANCE AND DECOLONIZATION

While there is much evidence substantiating the Aboriginal perspective on colonization outlined above, it is also true that Aboriginal people have resisted these processes ever since they were introduced by Amer-Europeans. Paulo Freire (1993) notes three obstacles that Aboriginal people face when resisting and/or decolonizing. The first obstacles is duality—desiring and fearing freedom and authenticity. In other words, Aboriginal persons want to be themselves fully; yet they do not want to leave the safety and familiarity of and conformity with their states of unfreedom. There is a pull in one direction for Aboriginal people to be true to their Aboriginal identity and culture, while a pull in the opposite direction causes them to be complacent with the images and systems bestowed upon them. The second obstacle is the internalization of the oppressor's consciousness—to the point where the oppressors' way of being human is desired as it is seen as real. After years, if not decades, of hearing the oppressors' messages that the best and most appropriate way of living is the oppressor's way, Aboriginal people come to hold the message dearly. They strive to be like the oppressor and even loath their own Aboriginalness. The third obstacle is that oppressive reality absorbs those within it and submerges human consciousness, thus creating domesticating behaviours and eliminating critical thinking and reflection. No longer seeking their own existence as peoples, Aboriginal persons give up questioning the system imposed upon them, and instead seek to live within it.

What is required to address these barriers and to resist colonial oppression is praxis. Praxis involves consciousness and action:

> In order for the oppressed to be able to wage the struggle for their liberation, they must perceive the reality of the oppression not as a closed world from which there is no exit, but as a limiting situation which they can transform. This perception is a necessary but not sufficient condition for liberation; it must become the motivating force for liberation action.... The oppressed can overcome the contradiction in which they are caught only when this perception enlists them in the struggle to free themselves. (Freire 1993: 31)

This consciousness and action should be sought at all levels: individual, family, community and nation.

On an emotional level, colonized individuals have to legitimize our feelings by validating them. Validating feelings requires us to internally experience them without inhibitions and to express them on our own terms. In terms of our physical selves, we must see and take pride in our image. This pride is demonstrated through means such as accepting our appearance, eating properly, taking precautions to protect ourselves from physical harm, including diseases, and staying physically active. On a mental level, we have to develop an awareness of our lives in respect to the colonial oppression we have faced. We must learn about our personal and our peoples' histories. Our knowledge of the oppression we have each experienced has to be acknowledged by ourselves as real. These experiences need to be validated by ourselves and others who have been oppressed in similar ways. We have to recapture our peoples' language, history and understanding of the world, take and live those teachings which will support us in this attempt to overcome oppression and reach *mino-pimatisiwin*[2] —the good life. On a spiritual level, we must learn and understand the values and beliefs of our people and freely decide those which we will internalize. We must validate these values and beliefs through our spiritual expression and daily practices.

Aboriginal families and communities, using the values and beliefs of our peoples, that we have freely chosen to exercise, must relearn how to be together in relationships. Our people must use our energy, power and abilities in ways which support and benefit our families and communities. Couples must find balance in their relationships and learn how to support one another in their attempts to reach *mino-pimatisiwin*. This requires getting rid of such negative influences as resentment, jealousy, negative attitudes and feelings of inferiority. Instead, couples can be respectful, supportive, encouraging, patient and listen and communicate effectively. Parents need to relearn how to parent in ways which reflect and/or respect the cultural values and beliefs they chose to internalize. They must model these values and beliefs to their children in all their actions so that the children can incorporate them in their interactions with one another. Children must once again be placed in the centre of the family, community and nation. The once supportive role of the extended family must be recognized and incorporated as part of each family's and community's attempt to overcome internalized colonization and to reach *mino-pimatisiwin*. Thus, competition within extended families and between families must be stopped and replaced with encouragement. Self-gratification, envy and jealousy must be replaced with support and a commitment to one another.

Communities must join and/or support one another as nations. This includes reflecting, discussing and incorporating the peoples' languages, values and beliefs in laws and governance for and over ourselves, respecting and following the laws established, and establishing leaders and systems which are directly answerable to the people, not to outside authorities. The communities' and nations' economic development must include a focus on the well-being of the people, including the seven generations to come, in a way which will honour the values and beliefs given to the people by generations who have moved on. The peoples' cultures must be relearned, supported and practised in ways that respect past and future generations of the people and which are relevant to the people today. Social institutions, such as justice, education, health, recreation and spiritual systems, must be developed and based upon the languages, values and beliefs of the people. Judicial systems must be developed to make the laws developed by the people a reality. Education systems must teach the peoples' own histories, ways of knowing and learning, languages, literature, arts and sciences, as well as the global histories and teachings from other peoples. The health system must incorporate the peoples' understanding of holistic health and therefore incorporate traditional practices of our healers and herbal remedies. Recreation programs should include activities that reflect the cultural values, including cooperative games, songs based upon our own languages, traditional dances and art that is based in the hearts of emancipated individuals. The people must relearn the meaning of the spiritual practices of the previous generations. These practices must be recognized and respected as a bonding force between individuals, families, communities, nations, the ancestors, the land and the universe. Ceremonies and rituals, as direct reflections of these connections and the values and beliefs of the people, must be supported for the well-being of the people.

In other words, our people must relearn what it means to be ourselves, whether Cree, Anishinaabe, Dakota, Mi'kmaq, Haida, Inuit or any of the other peoples. This understanding then needs to be implemented in all aspects of our lives. Most importantly, it must be implemented in ways which do not maintain or repeat the colonial processes that are based upon greed, self-righteousness and dominion over others. These must be resisted not only as they are forced upon us but as they exude from us.

The Role of an Aboriginal Approach

After speaking with the second professor mentioned earlier, I remembered part of a story Eddie once told me. It was about the only time his grandfather scolded him. His grandfather said, "The least little bit you hate, you are wrong." Because the encounters with the two professors caused me to have such strong feelings, I realized that I needed to reflect upon my feelings and experiences and come to an understanding of the situation. It was not until I took the time to reflect that I fully understood why my heart sank and why I hated what I was experiencing. Neither of these individuals were aware that our Elders have been speaking for decades, if not centuries, about the relationships between individuals, families, communities, nations and the world around them. They did not recognize that our views of the world are based upon these relationships and the wholeness of the universe, and that when we help one another, it is from this perspective. They did not realize that the "ecological" approach, which was first discussed in social work in the late 1970s, was really an infant to Aboriginal ways or that these diagrams were developed and presented before the ecological approach was ever acknowledged in social work. My heart sank because as much as they were able to learn about our ways, they were not quite able to grasp our realities, views and practices. I hated it because once again our views were being taken and reinterpreted instead of being accepted for what they were. Our people, our Elders in particular, were once again being ignored and pushed aside.

Colonialism in the helping professions is so discreet, as it hides behind its altruism and ignorance. Yet, it is found in all aspect of the professions. Whether it is in the historical perspectives, values and beliefs that Amer-European individuals bring with them to the educational institutes; or the teaching methodologies followed in the lecture halls and classrooms; or the theories and practices that are taught in these institutions; or in the conversations between a professor and an Aboriginal person, Amer-European colonialism remains present. In light of this presence, I was left with a question after these two encounters. If resistance and decolonization involves coming to know ourselves, our histories and our worldviews, how can we expect to develop this knowledge by relying upon the very people, regardless of their altruism, who oppress these aspects of our being?

The way out of this conundrum lies in applying the concept of praxis to our helping practices. This requires, at least, efforts by Aboriginal peoples in several areas, specifically our helping philosophies, research, education and practice. We need to turn to our traditional healers and Elders to relearn our helping philosophies. We need to relate these philosophies to the concerns and issues we face today as Aboriginal peoples. With the help of our healers and Elders, we need to build on these philosophies. In the area of research, we need to regenerate and use our own methods of research, as well as those outside methods which our people believe will contribute to our well-being. We need to train our own people to be researchers, ones who will be responsible to, and respectful of, Aboriginal peoples. In the area of education, we need Aboriginal instructors and professors. The teaching methods used should stem from and reflect Aboriginal peoples' views and practices, while the curriculum should be based upon Aboriginal peoples' philosophies and research. Aboriginal practitioners can use Aboriginal theories and approaches in their helping practices. In turn, these theories and approaches should be based upon the peoples' worldviews, beliefs and values.

In applying praxis to Aboriginal helping philosophies, research, education and practice, I am not suggesting that all Amer-European contributions to helping should be ignored or discarded. While I do believe that we need to hold Aboriginal perspectives and actions up front for Aboriginal people, I do not believe that we should solely follow a xenophobic response. As explained by Memmi (1991: 139), we may find ourselves before a counter-mythology that will only serve to maintain our oppression:

> The negative myth thrust on him [us] by the colonizer is succeeded by a positive myth about himself suggested by the colonized.... The colonized's [our] self-assertion, born out of a protest, continues to define itself in relation to it. In the midst of revolt, the colonized continues to think, feel and live against and, therefore, in relation to the colonizer and colonization.

We need to be willing to look at what other societies of the world, including Amer-European societies, have contributed. Through our worldviews, values and beliefs, we can use those aspects which will support us in our healing and which work in harmony with us as peoples and as individuals. Nor does this mean that Amer-Europeans should be excluded from these processes. While decolonization must come from Aboriginal people, the colonizer must develop awareness of how they maintain colonization, including awareness of the relationship between colonization and the helping professions, processes and institutions. They each must develop their own centredness, or as Memmi (1991) says, their personal sense of "humanism," and free themselves from their own enslavement to the oppressive system, including their denial, ignorance and self-righteousness. Above all, Amer-Europeans must not direct Aboriginal peoples in our resistance and decolonization. They must learn how to work in a new relationship with Aboriginal people, where Aboriginal people maintain the freedom to determine our own lives, including our own helping theories, approaches and practices.

It is in this light that the outline of the Aboriginal approach is offered as a small contribution to these tasks. Thus, this approach is an attempt at decolonization and resistance. It is an act of decolonization in that it serves to inform those previously unaware, or barely aware, that we have our own worldviews, beliefs, values and practices and that, despite efforts to bury them, they are ready to be put into practice. It is an act of resistance in that it attempts to maintain and support a grasp on our helping philosophies and practices. This resistance is multiplied when Aboriginal helpers incorporate the approach into their practices with Aboriginal people and in ways which respect the nation of the people with whom they are working.

It is my hope that presenting this Aboriginal approach will encourage and support others to reflect upon and investigate Aboriginal peoples' helping philosophies and practices. It will be through this reflection and investigation that individuals will be able to determine its usefulness to them and their peoples. I am certain that they will find my focus upon Aboriginal people as a group, as opposed to Cree peoples, of which I am one, to be the second greatest limitation to the Aboriginal approach (the first being my inability to speak Cree fluently). However, I am also certain that this and other limits will encourage the critical review of this Aboriginal approach. If nothing else, I hope that this critical review will support and encourage Aboriginal people to draw out those aspects of this approach that applies to the realities of their peoples. Moreover, I hope this critical review encourages Aboriginal people to push forward in unveiling, investigating, developing, sharing and practising other general and specific Aboriginal theories and approaches. In this way, we all may contribute to the demise of colonization.

Notes

1. The colonial processes identified here are not meant to disrespect the many leaders who have fought, politically or otherwise, on behalf of our people. In fact, as peoples we are rich with community and national leaders who were or are positive role models for us. I believe that without them our continuing attempts to emancipate ourselves as individuals and peoples would likely have ended long ago. As such, I also believe that we need to constantly highlight the resistence of our people and the leaders of such resistence in order to guide and maintain our resistive actions today. Perhaps that will be the focus of other books written by our people.
2. The term *mino-pimatisiwin* will be more fully defined in Chapter three.

CHAPTER THREE

FOUNDATIONS OF
AN ABORIGINAL APPROACH

A MEDICINE WHEEL BACKGROUND

When I set out to determine what an Aboriginal approach to social work and helping might be, I turned to a symbolic model that is frequently used by many Aboriginal peoples, namely the medicine wheel. It has been utilized to explain and address several issues, including racism (Calliou 1995), the impact of residential schools (Assembly of First Nations 1994), healing (Coggins 1990; Regnier 1994), sexual abuse (Hollow Water Community Holistic Circle Healing 1993), education (Odjig White 1996) and research (Young 1999). Its application is general and far-reaching. It is this wide application that made the medicine wheel appropriate to act as the guide for this approach.

The medicine wheel is an ancient symbol of the universe used to help people understand things or ideas which often cannot be seen physically. It reflects the cosmic order and the unity of all things in the universe. Indeed, it can be expressed in many ways as there is no absolute version of the wheel. On one level, many Aboriginal peoples, for example, the Anishinaabe, Cree and Dakota, have utilized the medicine wheel and given it their interpretations. On another level, individuals utilize the medicine wheel to reflect their understanding of themselves. I have also heard traditional ceremonial leaders explain that every person has their own medicine wheel since it can reflect each person's own life. Despite these variations, the medicine wheel has generally been constructed as a circle with four equal pie-shaped sections formed by four equidistant points connected by two perpendicular lines crossing in the middle of the circle. As a central symbol used for understanding various issues and perspectives, the medicine wheel reflects several key and interrelated concepts that are common to many Aboriginal methods of helping and healing. It is these concepts which are the foundation to this Aboriginal approach to social work.

In addition to these foundational concepts, there are several other components to this approach. These include values and perceptions which are based upon the worldviews of Aboriginal peoples, and, as such, they guide this Aboriginal approach's orientation. The components include qualities that support the helping process and characteristics held by the helper. These qualities and characteristics direct the approach to be more appropriate, consistent and effective for helping Aboriginal people.

The Foundational Concepts

The first foundational concept is of wholeness. In order to understand this concept, it is important to recognize that the medicine wheel has been used to symbolize many relating ideas and/or entities that can be expressed in sets of four and represented by the four cardinal directions—east, south, west and north. The symbolic importance of the cardinal directions to wholeness is pivotal:

> Wherever one stands in the world, there are always four equal directions. Without all the directions, the world is incomplete and cannot be. It is the unity of these directions that makes the whole a reality. Each direction relies on the existence of the other directions for its own identity as a direction. Each direction reflects differences in the world (plenitude) and sets out the possibility for interconnectedness. (Regnier 1994: 132)

Some easily recognizable examples of ideas and/or entities that are often cited by Aboriginal people include the four aspects of humanness—the emotional, physical, mental and spiritual—and the four key periods of the life cycle spanning from birth/infancy, to youth, to adulthood and finishing with elderhood/death. Other examples include the four races of people, represented by the colours red, yellow, black and white; the four primary elements of fire, water, wind (air) and earth; and the seasons of spring, summer, fall and winter. Each of these entities and/or ideas are part of a single whole.

Wholeness requires that we try to understand each part of the medicine wheel by understanding how it is connected to all other parts. Regnier (1994: 132–33) reflects this need for holistic attention:

> Wholeness in the cycle of the year requires movement through all seasons, wholeness in life requires movement through the phases of a human life, and wholeness in human growth requires the development of all aspects. The year-life and human growth can come to completion through this movement to wholeness. This movement to wholeness is natural and fundamental to all living things.

Thus, wholeness is the incorporation of all aspects of life and the giving of attention and energy to each aspect within ourselves and the universe around us. This giving of energy and attention requires balance.

Balance, the second foundational concept, implies that each part of the whole requires attention in a manner where one part is not focused upon to the detriment of the other parts (Clarkson, Morrissette and Regallet 1992; Young, Ingram and Swartz 1989). Balance occurs when a person is at peace and harmony within their physical, emotional, mental and spiritual humanness; with others in their family, community and the nation; and with all other living things, including the earth and natural world (Longclaws 1994; Malloch 1989; Zieba 1990). While balance is periodically and momentarily achieved, it is never achieved for an indefinitely extended period of time. The reality that life is ever-changing requires all beings to readjust in the constant pursuit to regain a sense of balance. While in this pursuit, we may give unequal focus on one part of the medicine wheel. Such imbalance is considered the source of disease or problems (Canda 1983; Guay 1994; Malloch 1989; Ross 1996). People who are in an ongoing state of imbalance will not be able to develop their full potential (Bopp et al. 1985). In order to restore balance, each part of the medicine wheel must be re-addressed in relation to one another. Peat (1994: 167) clearly explains this balancing of the four directions in relation to a four-legged chair:

> So it is with our four-legged chair. Any three of the legs will define a perfectly flat plane where the chair is in balance; the fourth leg will either be too long or too short. And this means that there will be different orientations for the chair in which three of the tips touch the floor while the fourth remains in the air. When you sit on the chair you wobble between these different balance points. This example demonstrates that the very sensitive and difficult process of achieving balance is a fundamental property of space, the universe, and the number four.... Achieving a final balance involves a dynamic process of constant adjustment.

On an intra-individual level, this means people must develop each aspect of themselves, the physical, emotional, mental and spiritual. On an inter-individual level, people must strive for their personal wellness in a manner which does not limit the wellness of others around them, including their family and community. On an inter-being level, this requires ensuring that the wellness of all beings is supported.

Balance involves more than just paying attention to each part of the medicine wheel. Balance includes giving attention to what connects each part of the medicine wheel. This brings us to the foundational concept of connection: the relationships between all the parts. Ross notes the extent to which these connections are emphasized: "Everything the healers explore seems to boil down to one issue: connection and disconnection. It's as if *some state of disconnection* (or unhealthy connection leading to a desire to be disconnected) *is assumed to be the cause of the problem*" (1996: 135, emphasis in original). Others state that people are imbedded in interconnections where they are not only relating to one another, but more accurately they are in relationship with all the other people at once (Janzen, Skakum and Lightning 1994; Nelson, Kelly and McPherson 1985; Pepper and Henry 1991; Wilkinson 1980). It is suggested that relationships are also made with "other than human beings"[1] and that these relationships are essential to a person's well-being (Aiken 1990; Hallowell 1992; Zieba 1990). Others emphasize that there is just as much concern and attention given to looking at connections within individuals, such as the relationship between an individual's mental and emotional wellness. Thus, in order to achieve balance, people need to constantly foster the relationships between entities outside of, as well as within, themselves. This fostering of relationships is central to harmony, the next foundational concept.

Harmony is frequently mentioned as a key concept to be achieved, whether it is with others (Brant 1990; Ellison-Williams and Ellison 1996; Herring 1996), in the world (Attneave 1982; Canda 1983), in the universe (Regnier 1994; Johnston 1976), for a good life (Dion Buffalo 1990; Longclaws 1994) or within one's self (Odjig White 1996). Herb Nabigon (no date: 49) shared a personal life story outlining how harmony was defined for him:

> A long time ago, my grandmother told me that the earth is our garden. The Creator made this garden for us and it was up to us to live in harmony with our garden. When we take from Mother Earth to feed ourselves, we should always thank Mother Earth and the animals and put something back. The principle, "Whenever you take, you must also give," was what my grandmother was teaching. Grandfather, a trapper, never wasted anything that he killed. He used everything for his livelihood. He had tremendous respect for all the four-legged creatures. My father was the same way. He was very close to nature. Through his way of living, he

taught me the value of respect for nature, although I never paid attention to his teachings for many, many years. I am glad my grandfather and my father taught me the value of respecting nature.

Thus, as Nabigon suggests, harmony includes respect for one's relationships with others and within oneself, as well as the give and take between entities. It focuses on establishing peace with oneself and the life around (Longclaws, Rosebush and Barkwell 1993). It is a process involving the relationships of all the various powers, energies and beings of the cosmos and happens when everyone—human, animal, plant and planet—fulfils their obligations and goes about their proper business (Peat 1994). It requires people to live within the natural cycles that move life and to find a fit between the components of life through collaboration, sharing of what is available, cooperation and respect for all elements of life.

Harmony is directly connected to the foundational concept of growth. Optimally, growth includes the development of a person's body, heart, mind and spirit in a harmonious manner. It is a lifelong process which leads people to their true selves. All people have the capacity to grow and change. Growth is dependent upon people using their volition to develop their physical, emotional, spiritual and mental aspects (Bopp et al. 1985). Further, all of creation is constantly growing and changing, with the exception of the ongoing cycles that are ever present. Regnier (1994) and Longclaws (1994) view growth as movement through life cycles towards wholeness, balance, interdependence or connectedness and harmony with oneself and with other living things. Growth is represented as the movement towards the centre of the medicine wheel. Longclaws (1994) refers to the centre of the wheel as *oda aki*, which is an Anishinaabe term he has interpreted as meaning centredness. Absolon (1993) refers to the centre of the wheel as the sacred fire. For both Absolon and Longclaws, centred people are balanced, in harmony with creation, connected and whole: they are at an optimum place for growth.

The centred person is also at an optimum place for healing, another foundation concept. Healing is not only seen as the process of recovering from an illness or problem. Indeed, these concerns are broadly re-conceptualized as disconnections, imbalances and disharmony. Healing is also viewed as a journey; it is something that people practise daily throughout their lives (Absolon 1993; Ross 1996). It is the broad transitional process "that restores the person, community, and nation to wholeness, connectedness, and balance" (Regnier 1994:135).

Healing is not only necessary for the individual, but it is also important for everyone around that person since we are all interconnected and have influence on each other (Longclaws 1994). Indeed, holistic healing involves the individual, the family and the community (Morrisseau 1998). However, as suggested by Aiken (1990: 24), healing for an individual begins with that individual: "The old Indian way of healing was first to know the illness and to know one's self. And because the individual participates in the healing process it is essential that a person needed to know themselves, their innermost core, their innermost spirit and soul, their innermost strength." As such, healing is also about people taking responsibility for their own learning and growth (Ross 1996).

It is through the taking of responsibility for their own personal healing and growth that individuals will be able to attain *mino-pimatisiwin* (Cree)—the good life. *Mino-pimatisiwin* is seen by many people as the overall goal of healing, learning and life in general (Aiken 1990; Bopp et al. 1985; Cajete 1994; Longclaws 1994; Longclaws et al. 1993; Hallowell 1992; Ross 1996). Rose Auger (1994: 138), a Cree Elder, says that people need to take responsibility to reach *mino-pimatisiwin*. She states:

> When you choose to make your life good, it will be good.... The Creator gave you a sound mind and an incredible spirit and a way of being so that you can do anything right now! You can change that attitude same as you wake up in the morning and it's a new day. Your mind and everything else can be new. I've lived through hardship and horror, and I'm a loving, caring, and giving person because I choose to be that way. I choose to listen to the other side to guide me.

This growth and attempt to reach the good life is not just an individual focus. It also involves the family and community. Herring (1996: 74) indirectly supports this point when he speaks of self-actualization in a manner which reflects the idea of families and communities reaching *mino-pimatisiwin*. He suggests that "Native cultures emphasize cooperation, harmony, interdependence, the achievement of socially oriented and group goals, and collective responsibility. Thus the goal [of self actualization] is more akin to family and tribal self-actualization."

KEY SUPPORTING VALUES

All cultures have values. Gaywish (2000) notes nine value categories that are commonly used across many Aboriginal cultures: (1) vision/wholeness; spirit-centred, (2) respect/harmony, (3) kindness, (4) honesty/integrity, (5) sharing, (6) strength, (7) bravery/courage, (8) wisdom and (9) respect/ humility. Cajete (1999) discusses several idealized values as being the core to Aboriginal cultures. These include respecting individual differences, quietness, patience, an open work ethic, mutualism as expressed through cooperation, a nonverbal orientation, an emphasis on seeing and listening, a relative time orientation, practicality, a holistic orientation, spirituality and a tendency towards caution. The Anishinaabe people emphasize that the values that are to be cherished include wisdom, love, respect, bravery, honesty, humility and truth. Several authors, including myself, have spoken with Cree Elders who outline particular values to be held by people. These include respect, caring, faith, honesty, kindness and sharing. On the other hand, there are some opposing conditions that stem from an individual's fears and which affect a person's ability to reach a good life. These conditions include envy, resentment, not caring, jealousy, a negative attitude and feeling inferior (Absolon 1993; Briks 1983; Nabigon 1993). One of these Cree Elders, Joe Cardinal, suggests how these opposing forces be addressed: "If the positive aspects of the self are taken care of, the negative side will die a natural death" (cited in Meili 1991: 253).

Several values are highlighted in this Aboriginal approach as important concepts since they support one to reach *mino-pimatisiwin*. Sharing is one of these values. It has been mentioned extensively by many writers (Auger 1994; Boldt and Long 1984; Brant 1990; Hamilton and Sinclair 1991; Nabigon no date) and by Elders during my discussions with them. As O'Meara (1996) notes, practical and sacred knowledge, life experiences and food reflect the wide variety of things shared between people. She further notes that sharing is the most natural way of developing human relationships. Smith Attimoyoo, a Cree/Saulteaux Elder, gave his thoughts on sharing through an example at the Plains Cree Conference in 1975:

> We may have a little piece of bannock, the only piece in the cupboard. We don't say, "Well I'm going to save this for tomorrow, I may want this tomorrow." But instead my mother or my wife, makes that tea and serves this little piece of bannock that she has. That's the kind of sharing that we have to take to our young people so that once again they may be able to tell the values that

we have, to maintain this sharing and this living together. (cited in Canadian Plains Research Centre 1979: 52)

Sharing is tied to equality and democracy in that every person is considered as valuable as every other person and treated accordingly (Brant 1990). It also reduces conditions such as greed, envy and arrogance that may cause conflict within the group. Zieba (1990) suggests that sharing is viewed as so fundamentally important that any breach would result in sickness.

From the time I have spent with traditional healers and Elders, I have noted, as have many authors (Aiken 1990; Clarkson et al. 1992; Guay 1994; Morrisseau 1998; Nabigon no date; Nelson et al. 1985; Niezen 1993), that respect is another value emphasized as of key importance to Aboriginal people. Respect has been defined as showing honour and esteem or treating someone or something with deference and courtesy (Bopp et al. 1985). A respectful individual will not impose their views, particularly through judgement, onto another person. Discussing respect in wider terms, Calliou (1995: 67) identifies that "a premise of the First Nations world is that we unconditionally respect all beings because we all begin as seeds from the same materials of this Mother Earth. In the circle no one individual (two-legged, four-legged, mineral, plant, etc.) is deemed 'more than' or 'less than' another, so that treatment which elevates or denigrates one or the other is ruled out." Respect is a central responsibility in all relationships, including spiritual relationships (Hampton et al. 1995; Zieba 1990). Indeed, one Cree Elder shared with me that respect is such an important concept for Cree peoples, it is considered one of the foundations to the peoples' cultures (see also Briks 1983).

Another key value to this approach and one that is frequently raised and merits particular attention is spirituality (Aitken 1990; Anderson 2000; Bopp et al. 1985; Cajete 1999; Canadian Plains Research Centre 1979; Clarkson et al. 1992; Ermine 1995; Hampton et al. 1995; Longclaws 1994; Longclaws et al. 1993; Nabigon 1993; Peat 1994). Aboriginal philosophy and ways of knowing encompass spirituality to such a degree that it almost dictates the necessity of including spirituality in this approach. Such a necessity is clear in Cajete's comment that "all things and all thoughts are related through spirit" (1994: 44) and Ellison-Williams and Ellison's (1996) suggestion that healing involves the spiritual aspect of people. Zieba (1990) confirms the role of spirituality in healing through his study of Aboriginal healers who were either herbalists, ritualists or charismatic Pentecostal healers. Therefore, the approach I present includes people's spirituality.

PERCEPTION OF PEOPLE

Many Aboriginal people believe, as does this approach, that humans are good by nature. It is also recognized that bad attributes and forces exist and are expressed by people (Absolon 1993; Attneave 1982; Waldram 1994). Since these negative forces in the universe seek to lead people away from their path and purpose in life, people have to actively strive to maintain this goodness and to develop themselves positively towards *mino-pimatisiwin* (Bopp et al. 1985; Dugan 1985; Longclaws 1994, Regnier 1994). In following their path, people are orientated to finding their true nature. They are also nurturing the experience of being alive since they are finding, seeing and accepting the goodness in all life around them. It is these processes that support the view that while people are mainly in the state of *being*—the experience of being alive and seeing the goodness in all life as it is experienced—they are also in a state of *being-in-becoming*—the active seeking of one's purpose. Aiken (1990: 34) suggests this in his reflection that, "in the Indian world a really happy and full life is gained by living within each moment and taking it in your life's journey. And thus each moment does not have an end, but it may continue to live within us and to enrich us."

These orientations of being and being-in-becoming suggest that Aboriginal people are present and future time orientated. However, for Aboriginal people, "life is experienced as a series of circles, in which change is not an irreversible line, but a curve bending backwards toward its beginning. Time extends from far in the past to far into the future" (Nelson et al. 1985: 237). Brant reflects on the time orientation of Aboriginal people as well, stating that "the Native person has an intuitive, personal and flexible concept of time" (1990: 536). In light of these points, this approach holds that past personal and generational experiences are important, as well as that present events will affect future generations (Benton-Banai 1988; Clarkson et al. 1992; Ridington 1982).

Another concept associated with the perception of people is how relationships are viewed. According to Johnston (1976) and Ross (1996), relationships are seen as highly significant to each person's well-being and purpose, since people influence, and are influenced by, relationships. Ross recognizes that the attempt to accommodate those relationships which lie between and within entities (people and things) "instead of dominating the things within them—seems to lie at the heart of a great many Aboriginal approaches to life" (1996: 63).

Relationships are guided by good conduct, since good conduct leads to *mino-pimatisiwin* (Hallowell 1992). One aspect of good conduct involves not interfering in and not judging the affairs of others, since interference and judgements limit a person's self-determination (Janzen et al. 1994; Good Tracks 1989). It is also believed that through non interference and non-judgment positive interrelationships are encouraged (Brant 1990). Elder Jim Canipitatao, (speaking in Cree), emphasized the importance of non-interference in relationships: "We must help each other. We must help each other and ask for God's help to understand each other, love each other and help each other. It is useless to confront each other, my relatives. It is better to ask for unity, to work together, to think of our grandchildren. This is the Cree way" (English interpretation cited in Canadian Plains Research Centre 1979: 43).

In this Aboriginal approach, there are particular ways of understanding the relationships people hold. Of primary importance is understanding the sacredness of children. In one of my discussions with a Cree Elder, *awasisak*—children—were described as "the meaning of life." Holding the centre spot in the circle of humanity, children help people to see their purpose and to recognize their responsibilities to the many generations to come. People are also encouraged to see their responsibility to the previous generations by turning to the teachings passed on by them. From these teachings, people come to understand how to nurture life and that children are to be cherished as teachers from whom all parents must learn. Thus, in an Aboriginal approach, people are supported to hold children as sacred and to learn from their relationship with them.

Another important relationship for people is the one between women and men. Traditionally, Aboriginal societies depended upon the contributions made by both women and men. While they often had different roles and commitments, women and men were equally important to the well-being of the people. To devalue one gender was to devalue your society and in turn yourself. In particular, as women were the life-givers through birthing, they were held to be closer to the Creator. Men had to work at developing this closeness since they could never understand creation as closely as women understood it. Further, as the life-givers to a most sacred gift bestowed upon a family and community—the children—women were to be highly respected.

It is recognized by those utilizing this Aboriginal approach that the foundational concepts must be followed in the relationships between women and men. Both have to be acknowledged as having a purpose and as part of the whole. There has to be balance between men and women in that one cannot be focused upon to the detriment of the other. The relationship between women and men has to be nurtured in a way that both are harmoniously supporting each other in their attempts to reach *mino-pimatisiwin*. Each gender must respect the other and the other's understanding of what is necessary to strive towards *mino-pimatisiwin*. This understanding comes about through the sharing between the genders, not domination and oppression of one over the other. In following this way, women and men, whether in a couple relationship or otherwise, can support the other's healing, learning and growth.

The relationship people hold with the land is also important. Many traditional Aboriginal peoples' spirituality includes an intimate relationship with the land. As Belinda Vandenbroeck (1998: xiii) states, "We all need to remember that the spirit of the land is connected to the spirit within each of us which in turn connects us to the Creator. There has never been a separation from this, even when our culture was at its ebb." She emphasizes that we need to coexist in harmony with the land, Mother Earth. Vine Deloria expresses concern about how we are presently relating to the land:

> Today we rely entirely too much upon the artificial universe that we have created, the world of machines and electricity. In most respects we have been trained to merge our emotions and beliefs so that they mesh with the machines and institutions of the civilized world.... In our electronic/electric, mechanical world, we rely on instruments of our own construction to enable us to relate to the rest of the world ... consequently we attribute to landscape only the aesthetic and not the sacred perspective. (1999: 257)

In recognizing the need to overcome an objectification of the land, an Aboriginal approach encourages people to re-establish a connection to the land. Such a reconnection helps people to see life in a broader sense that incorporates both the physical and spiritual realms. All the foundational concepts can be observed and learned through this connection. It also helps people in their journey to *mino-pimatisiwin* since establishing these connections are part of the centring processes.

PERCEPTIONS OF PEOPLE'S FUNCTIONING

Several factors are seen to significantly influence a person's functioning. The first of these is history. It is clear that Aboriginal peoples' histories have and continue to greatly affect them (Duran and Duran 1995; Janzen et al. 1994; LaDue 1994; Morrissette et al. 1993). Of all the events that have occurred, the process and effects of colonization have influenced all facets of Aboriginal people's lives on various levels, including the national, communal, familial and individual. This Aboriginal approach recognizes and incorporates the need to understand the process and effects of colonization on all facets and levels. It also sees the need to highlight Aboriginal peoples' histories as a structured relationship and as a personal experience (Morrissette et al. 1993). Of the many facets, within an individual and within the people, it is suggested that the spiritual aspect has suffered the greatest stress from colonization and that this aspect requires special attention (McKenzie and Morrissette 1993).

Equally important as the effects of history on people's functioning is the cyclical nature of life. This cycle is viewed in relation to the medicine wheel, where life is seen as having four key phases—child, youth, adult, elder (Bopp et al. 1985; Calliou 1995; Guay 1994). Within each phase there are tasks that are developed as ones seeks *mino-pimatisiwin*. These tasks are not limited to particular phases in life but are ever present for people to address throughout their lifetime. Bopp et al. (1985: 40) warns against a fixed focus:

> Certainly, the fundamental value of this tool (the medicine wheel) is a way of measuring our own progress and development, and a means for assessing what we must work on next in our journey through life. One final warning is needed. It is dangerous to categorize yourself as a "northern person" or a "eastern person." In order to use the wheel correctly, you must visualize yourself in the centre of the wheel, connected equally to all points by the power of your will.… What we are really doing is using the patterns found in nature … to understand our own selves.

Thus, while it is possible to describe particular developments and achievements in relation to particular life stages (Longclaws et al. 1993; Longclaws 1994), these phases are primarily significant to people individually so that they may be able to better understand their own development.

Another function that is perceived by this approach as being important for understanding a person's development are the states of consciousness and unconsciousness. There has been great attention given to the unconscious via spirits, altered states, dreams and visions (Dugan 1985; Dusenberry 1962; Hallowell 1992; Irwin 1994; McPherson and Rabb 1993; Niezen 1993; Peat 1994; Tofoya 1989; Waldram 1994). Dion Buffalo (1990) recognizes the importance of the unconscious for the Plains

Cree. She states that individuals heal by bringing the unconscious conflict and resistance to a conscious level where they can work with the issues. Often this process incorporates spiritual dimensions that are reached through dreams and visions. Among the traditional Plains peoples, dreams are given a strong priority and are a source of knowledge and power (Irwin 1994). It is through dreams that they are able to reach their *pawakanak*—spiritual beings who offer guidance (Dunsenberry 1962). Hallowell (1992) goes further, saying that by contacting their spiritual helpers through their dreams, the Anishinaabe people's ability to reach *mino-pimatisiwin* was enhanced.

Similar observations are made of the vision quest. It is suggested that a vision is initiated for two reasons: first, when people are approaching a significant moment or undertaking in their lives, and second, when they feel a need for help beyond human power in order to cope with what is to come. It is believed by the Cree people that pursuing inner visions can lead to enhancing one's self physically, mentally and spiritually (Ferrara 1999). It has also been suggested that "one of the principle motives for a person to undertake a vision quest was to discover direction and meaning for his life. This search had always included the communal dimension, for it was especially true in Indian [Aboriginal] society that the individual was defined in the context of the Tribe" (Dugan 1985: 156). Ermine reviews this process of learning, securing power, enhancement and help through such events as dreams and vision, a process the Cree people refer to as *mamatowisowin*:

> In their quest to find meaning in the outer space, Aboriginal people turned to the inner space. This inner space is the universe of being within each person that is synonymous with the soul, the spirit, the self, or the being. The priceless core within each of us and the process of touching that essence is what Kierkegaard called inwardness. Aboriginal people found a wholeness that permeated inwardness and that also extended into the outer space. Their fundamental insight was that all existence was connected and that the whole enmeshed the being in its inclusiveness. In the Aboriginal mind, therefore, an immanence is present that gives meaning to existence and forms the starting point for Aboriginal epistemology. (1995: 103)

In light of their importance, this approach gives credence to the influence of dreams and visions on functioning. It recognizes that Aboriginal philosophy is a spiritual philosophy that strongly incorporates both the conscious and unconscious and that the inward looking processes associated with the unconscious is not only important for individuals, but for the community (Aiken 1990).

Also important to people's functioning is the concept of change, which is viewed in a particular manner by Aboriginal people in that it is tied to balance, relationships and harmony. Aboriginal peoples see the universe as being in a constant state of flux, where an order of alliances, compacts and relationships between the energies and spirits exists (Little Bear 1998; Peat 1994). This order, being in flux, is always in a state of transition between order and chaos. As such, balance lies in flux, transition and change. In parallel with this transitional view, Chief Simon Baker (cited in Baker and Kirkness 1994) suggests that change occurs in cycles. Changes are continuous in that people are always involved in transitional processes either directly or indirectly. These transitional processes may be initiated from sources external to the individual, such as when a storm strikes or a family members moves away, or from within an individual, such as when a person experiences overwhelming fear or a new understanding of their self. At times, changes are required, particularly when individuals are not balanced within, are disconnected in their relationships or are in disharmony with their environment. Even when a person finds a balanced, centred state and attempts to remain "stuck" in this state, their growth is hindered since the world around them continues to change. This is emphasized in many Aboriginal trickster stories which describe how the trickster—such as *Wisahkecahk*—can be disruptive to the cycles and in doing so bring about new orders to the world. Thus, change is an ongoing transitional process of balancing and connecting relationships within the individual, among individuals and between individuals and the world around them (Longclaws 1994; Regnier 1994). This process is not limited to the individual but also involves relationships on familial, communal, tribal, national and universal levels (Briks 1983; LaDue 1994; Longclaws et al. 1993). As exemplified by the Mi'kmaw, Aboriginal peoples' way of being is "to be with the flux, to experience its changing form, and to develop a relationship with the forces, thus creating harmony" (Battiste and Henderson 2000: 79).

The primary motivation for people to change lies in their desire to reach *mino-pimatasiwin* (Aiken 1990; Hallowell 1992; Overholt and Callicott 1982). Therefore, the primary onus is on individuals to pursue changes in their own lives (Bopp et al. 1985; Ross 1996). Ross emphasizes this personal responsibility for change:

> Only you can find the will to take those first steps towards trusting others, towards taking hold of the hands that reach down to help you. The healers can show you how they trust each other, how they don't let go of each other, but they can't force you to reach out yourself. They can only demonstrate, teach, encourage and receive. Everything else must come from the individual who needs the healing. (1996: 190)

Similarly, the responsibility for a family, community, tribe or nation to make the changes needed to reach *mino-pimatisiwin* lies with that family, community, tribe or nation.

Related to the change process is the concept of power. In following the foundational concepts, power is viewed as something that exists in all living entities. For people, power is tied to their volition—their ability to imagine something or make a choice and to implement the actions to make that image or choice a reality. When the cycles directly involving people are in harmony, people are utilizing their volition—hence power— to help themselves heal, learn and grow. Cyclically, this leads people to a greater access to power and can also support other people in their healing, learning and growth. Thus, it is recognized that levels of power held by people—indeed, all living entities—vary, depending upon the spiritual and physical resources available to them and their ability to tap into these resources. This varying distribution of power between individuals is accepted as long as the power is used to contribute to the creation and the maintenance of balance, relationships and harmony. Indeed, the greater power an individual holds, the greater is the responsibility for that person to contribute to the well-being of others.

Power is abused when an individual, for their own gain, hinders or attempts to hinder another person's or entities's learning, healing and/or growth. In other words, they stop individuals from following their own journey. Abuses of power result in imbalance, disconnections and disharmony. As demonstrated in many trickster stories, when an individual or entity continuously reaps the power of others for self gain, ultimately there will be a change in the processes, which then moves the distribution of power towards a more balanced, harmonious state. This change may come from within the entities themselves or by force through external sources. Until that time of significant change to the processes, the individual or entity may appear to be growing more powerful. The reality of the larger picture is that there is little growth; there may even be deterioration.

HELPING RELATIONSHIPS

As in therapy, in an Aboriginal approach to social work and other helping professions, emphasis is given to the relationships of the people being helped, since these affect people's existence in the world. In an Aboriginal approach, it is especially essential to nurture the relationship between the person being helped and the helper and to enhance its development and growth as a part of helping. Emphasizing relationships as the focus of the change process, Duran and Duran states:

> Any psychology [or helping practice] of Native American people must have a direct impact on the way that any type of relationship is experienced. The experience of therapy or healing is no exception to the experience of being in the world. The need for healing can be explained by the fact that the client/community has lost the ability to be in harmony with the life process of which the client/community is a part. (1995: 15)

More specifically, the focus of the helping process is the restoration of relationships that have become out of balance (Malloch 1989; Ross 1996). From a holistic perspective, it could be said that "an intervention will need to restore physical well-being to the body and harmony to the damaged social and spiritual relationships" (Ellison Williams and Ellison 1996: 148). LaDue (1994) notes the social aspect and that the focus can be on an individual, familial, community or national level of relationships. The level of relationships can be further extended to include people's relationships with the Creator and Mother Earth (Clarkson et al. 1992; McKenzie and Morrissette 1993). In an Aboriginal approach, the people offering help are required to focus on maintaining their own balance, connectedness and harmony—in other words, centredness—since they are in relationship with the people receiving help (Nelson et al. 1985). Indeed, it is emphasized that "before you can reach out to help the people around you, you must first understand how to help yourself" (Antone and Hill 1990: 7).

It is important that individuals utilizing an Aboriginal approach reflect upon their own lives and be willing to share their life experience to support the healing of others. Personal experience can be also used to demonstrate alternatives for healing (Nelson et al. 1985; Ross 1996). Thus, the helper understands that their life is a journey and that, within the helping relationship, their journey is in relation to the journey of each person they are helping. Through this self-reflective process, helpers are better able to recognize the learning and support required by those they are helping. Helpers are able to seek out the positive attributes in other peoples' lives and experiences. In turn, they are able to see and acknowledge the reciprocity in the helping relationship, since they will likely learn and receive support from the people with whom they are working.

Equally important to the approach is that healers live the life they wish for others (Katz and St. Denis 1991). They attempt to follow foundational concepts and strive for *mino-pimatisiwin*. Helpers are able to clearly identify their own values and to incorporate the values of sharing and respect into their lives. They acknowledge, respect and follow a spiritual life. This is particularly necessary since centredness involves the spiritual aspect of people and since the traditional Aboriginal helper role includes acting as a mediator between the physical and spiritual aspects of creation (Absolon 1993; Malloch 1989). They recognize how they are connected to the cycles around them and how these cycles are influencing them as helpers. They understand that fluxes and changes occur within these cycles and they are able to adjust to them.

People offering help recognize that they are not experts in the healing process since "there is no inherent distinction between the helper and the helped" (Nelson et al. 1985: 241). Humility, not judgement, is paramount in this process (Ross 1996). The helper is prepared "to sit patiently through long pauses and to listen rather than to be directive or to interrupt the speaker" (Broken Nose 1992: 384). Helpers are prepared for periods of silence (Attneave 1982), especially since they recognize that "coming-to-know arises out of silence" (Peat 1994: 75). Thus, the skills to be patient and a good listener are necessary since such a non-directive approach takes time. These skills are also related to another ability that should be developed: the art of speaking from the heart.

> Out of this power of silence great oratory is born. When Native people speak they are not talking from the head, relating some theory, mentioning what they have read in some book, or what someone else has told them. Rather, they are speaking from the heart, from the traditions of their people, and from the knowledge of their land; they speak of what they have seen and heard and touched, and of what has been passed on to them by the traditions of their people. (Peat 1994: 75)

Speaking from the heart also includes the attempt to reach and touch the listener's heart. This process honours the listener because the speaker is sharing something that is truly meaningful and not merely informational.

It is by reaching inward and speaking from their own heart that people are able to reach others. In the helping process, it shows genuineness, empathy and concern and brings people closer together in their common humanity.

The helping relationship is one where the helper and the person receiving the support are involved in a shared experience of learning and growing (Hampton et al. 1995), with the helper fundamentally a supporter involved in an interdependent relationship (Nelson et al. 1985). In order to respect individual autonomy, people offering help are non-coercive and include an indirect method in their practice (Longclaws 1994). As Boldt and Long (1984) point out, no human being rightfully has control over another's life. The Aboriginal conceptualization of non-interference stresses that it is inappropriate to decide for others or to coerce them into a course of action (Good Tracks 1989). This focus on personal autonomy and interdependence emphasizes that people have a personal responsibility for their own growth as well as for what they bring to the relationships they are involved in (Ross 1996). Many Aboriginal helping interventions that are parallel with social work and other helping professions involve a relationship of interdependence and support and tend to remain fairly indirect.

Unless the person has approached a traditional healer asking for a particular problem to be cured, the assessment of what a person is facing is completed by the person being helped (Nelson et al. 1985). Helpers may support this assessment process by raising the person's awareness of the wholeness of and interrelations within life. Since the Aboriginal approach outlined here espouses personal responsibility, the helper supports the person being helped in setting their own goals (Aiken 1990; Nelson et al. 1985). In this way, the people seeking help direct their own actions and take responsibility for reaching their own goals.

One technique that is frequently used in this Aboriginal approach is storytelling. In many Aboriginal societies, stories are often used as the vehicle for true understanding and to describe the way of healing, health and wholeness (Bruchac 1992; Cajete 1999; Dion Buffalo 1990; O'Meara 1996; Peat 1994). They serve to establish and confirm traditional beliefs, values and practice, which then act as guides for present behaviours (Bucko 1998). They require listeners to pay close attention.

> Our Grandfathers and Grandmothers—our Elders—tell us that it is not enough merely to listen to the stories which they tell: we must make every attempt to listen to the stories which they tell: we must make every attempt to understand the truths which are

embodied within these stories and myths. The truth must then become part of us, who have stopped to listen the inner truth ought to lead to self-actualization for the man or woman whom the story is told. (Asikinack 1995: 93)

Some situations may call for the helper to share experiential stories that directly relate to the situation being addressed. Others may call for the sharing of general stories, in a manner which allows individuals to personally discover whatever meaning in the story relates to them. For some peoples, such as the Cree, narratives are preferred over explanations of events in the form of simple facts (Ferrara 1999). Such a preference is understandable since storytelling easily follows the value of respect by incorporating a non-interfering approach (Gaywish 2000).

The use of humour is another important factor in the helping process. Indeed Aiken suggests that "humour to our people is probably one of the greatest medicinal strengths" (1990: 29). He considers it an indirect nurturing approach that is non-confrontational and non-interfering. Humour has been, and is, such a significant aspect of Aboriginal cultures that there are numerous stories based upon the antics of various clowns and tricksters (Peat 1994). Humourous stories are used for healing since they can "demonstrate the universal fallibility of contemporary existence" (Bucko 1998: 167). Humour supports the release of tension and energy. It supports knowledge development since much can be learned from the laughter stemming from particular situations. Gaywish (2000) also suggests that humour affirms culturally prescribed roles and relationships.

Role modelling is another process utilized in the helping process, particularly since it usually is indirect, non-confrontational and supportive (Brant 1990; McCormick 1995; Pepper and Henry 1991; Ross 1996). Strong role models serve to inspire others and support them to see their own potential to reach *mino-pimatisiwin*. Role modelling is tied to the process, "teacher as healer," which requires a person to live the life that is to be taught and wait for the student to come seeking knowledge. Cree people refer to this person as *okiskinohamakew*—"a person who teaches what he has learned from life and people ... one who serves as a guide" (Katz and St. Denis 1991: 31).

Referral to and the enlistment of the support of Elders are other helping processes related to role modelling. As suggested by Couture:

Elders are superb embodiments of highly developed human potential.... Their qualities of mind (intuition, intellect, memory, imagination) and emotion, their profound and refined moral sense manifest in an exquisite sense of humour, in a sense of caring and communication finesse in teaching and counselling, together with a high level of spiritual and psychic attainment, are perceived as clear behavioural indicators, deserving careful attention, if not compelling emulation. (1996: 47)

Elders are seen as individuals who understand themselves in relation to the universe around them and who have been able to centre themselves on a consistent basis. These well-respected people have the ability to transmit the culture (Baker and Kirkness 1994; Clarkson et al. 1992; Malloch 1989; Medicine 1987). This is highly significant since transmitting the culture is considered a key aspect of the healing process for Aboriginal people (LaDue 1994; Listening to the Elders: 2 1992; McKenzie and Morrissette 1993; Morrissette et al. 1993: Poproski 1997). They are also well prepared to provide counselling, act as key figures in unifying families, offer spiritual guidance and conduct ceremonies (Red Horse 1980; Stiegelbauer 1996; Waldram 1997). Overall, Elders are respected as sources of help because of their experiences and how they have learned from those experiences (Stiegelbauer 1996).

Ceremonies and rituals are significant in their own right (Aiken 1990; Benton-Banai 1988; Bucko 1998; Longclaws et al. 1993; McCormick 1995; Peat 1994; Regnier 1994; Ross 1996). Longclaws explains that (1994: 26) "ceremonies assist individuals in centring themselves and give them strength to participate in a lifelong learning process." From simple symbolic acts to highly organized contextual events involving many people, ceremonies cultivate the spirit and the spiritual (Cajete 1999). They include established traditions such as smudging and prayer, naming ceremonies, pipe ceremonies, sweat lodges, *wikkowin*—feasts for the dead (Cree), vision quests and *nipakwesimowin*—rain dances (Cree). Peat (1994) suggests that ceremonies are not rights to be exercised but obligations to be fulfiled in order for renewal in the life cycle.

Ceremonies facilitate healing for people. For example, Stoney medicine people lead sweat lodge ceremonies and offer prayers and other rituals as remedies for curing illnesses (Long and Fox 1996: 253). Ceremonies provide ways to discharge emotions through crying, yelling, talking, swearing, singing, dancing and praying (Ross 1996). Indeed, this discharge of emotion, in and of itself, is seen as a healing method (McCormick 1995). Cajete (1999: 59) also notes that "through symbolic use of prayer, song, dance, and communal activity, Native Americans developed highly creative techniques for guiding social behaviour and ethics. The social psychology inherent in ritual and ceremony provided powerful group empathy and cohesion which reinforced the social self-image of each individual participant." In a broader view, ceremonies are used to establish relationship with the essential forces in nature (Battiste and Henderson 2000: 78) Overall, ceremonies are significant and are to be regularly used, even by the healthiest people (Ross 1996).

To prepare themselves to follow these techniques and processes, helpers must go through certain experiences and hold certain characteristics and abilities. Similar to people who have learned to conduct healing ceremonies by going through years of intense study (LaDue 1994), helpers following an Aboriginal approach must study the life around them. This includes studying themselves, other people and how cyclical processes and lives are related. Certainly this studying is necessary since utilizing an Aboriginal approach will at least require some basic knowledge of and the ability to appropriately use the skills that reflect and respect Aboriginal worldviews and lifestyles.

NOTES

1. "Other than human beings" is a concept following Hallowell's description of beings of an additional class to the one the Anishinaabek use for themselves. He states (1992: 64), "The category includes animate beings to whom the Ojibwa [Anishinaabek] attribute essentially the same characteristics as themselves and whom I shall call "other than human" persons. This term is more descriptively appropriate than labelling this class of persons "spiritual" or "supernatural" beings, if we assume the viewpoint of the Ojibwa themselves."

CHAPTER FOUR

DEEPENING OUR UNDERSTANDING: TALKING WITH CONDUCTORS OF SHARING CIRCLES

Sharing circles are both helping techniques and processes which set the stage for people's ongoing healing, growth and self-development (Antone and Hill 1990). The general purpose of circles is to create a safe environment for people to share their views and experiences with one another (Guidelines for Talking Circles 1990). They have several goals, including the initiation of the healing process, promotion of understanding, joining with others and growth (Stevenson 1999: 10). An Aboriginal approach to social work and other helping practices is reflected in these techniques, processes and goals. By closely reviewing sharing circles as a representative of the many Aboriginal helping techniques and processes, we can begin to develop a greater understanding of the relationship between sharing circles and an Aboriginal approach. We can also come to a deeper understanding of how an Aboriginal approach applies to helping and healing.

This chapter supports the development of this understanding through a detailed overview of sharing circles. The first section of the chapter briefly addresses the connection between history and sharing circles. The second section introduces the first of four key elements Aboriginal people frequently focus upon, that being the physical aspect. Specifically, this section addresses the physical description, the participants, the conductor and the relational components of sharing circles. The third section addresses the remaining three elements: the emotional, mental and spiritual aspects of circles. The final section briefly outlines the connection between sharing circles and an Aboriginal approach to helping. By drawing out this connection, the essence of sharing circles—the support and encouragement of people to seek out *mino-pimatisiwin*—is acknowledged.

AN HISTORICAL JOURNEY INTO AN ABORIGINAL HELPING PROCESS

It was emphasized by Glen that "we need to recognize that Aboriginal people have been doing ceremonies for thousands of years" and that "in order to get across how important these things are you kind of need to do a little historical overview." Historically, Aboriginal ceremonies, council meetings and social gatherings included the circle format. Regnier explains:

> Sacred Circle accounts are passed from generation to generation through ceremonies, legends, and storytelling. Sacred Circle symbolism is enacted in meetings, sun dances, sweat lodges, sweet grass ceremonies, pipe ceremonies, and feasts where participants confer, celebrate, and pray. This symbol represents unity, interdependence, and harmony among all beings in the universe, and time as the continual recurrence of natural patterns. (1995: 316)

Sharing circles have been used for various purposes throughout Aboriginal peoples' histories, and most of the conductors with whom I spoke addressed this history. Fanny emphasized this when she stated that sharing circles have "always been here and they were very strong." Marg suggested that sharing circles were used for things such as arranging hunting expeditions and marriages and sharing information. She also stated that, "a long time ago we didn't have marriage counsellors. Sharing circles were used to strengthen a relationship's ties." Sharing circles were also utilized for addressing delinquency, to make decisions (Mary) and for spiritual gatherings where people prayed, sang and told stories (Fanny). Fanny recalled one of these circles that occurred many years ago:

> I remember my grandfather as a child. He took my brothers and me to a church. It was just a little Pentecostal church. There were benches in the church, you know, just rough benches. About six adults had gathered. Some brought instruments. These was a violin and a guitar. There was a small light, a kerosene lamp. They were sitting at the front of the church facing one another. I was there too, but I was lying down on one of the pews. So I guess that's why we have circles is because people face towards the centre, face each other. And when you get a group of people together there's no choice but to sit in a circle. So this small group of people would sing hymns and tell stories. I would be very tired but I'd get to hear the stories. They told scary stories … (laughter). They talked about seeing lights, you know, spirits. So that's what they were doing. They were sharing. So whenever anybody talked in between songs they told stories. I liked it because they would tell some of those very exciting, maybe a little scary, stories and I would be on that trip with them. So I

think talking circles been around forever. Since the beginning of time.

Longclaws (1994) notes that this passing down of circle symbolism and the enactment of the circle in ceremonies, including sharing circles, continues. As the use of circles has been, and continues to be, a significant part of Aboriginal helping processes, by coming to understand sharing circles in greater detail it is possible to develop a greater understanding of these processes.

Glen and Bernie emphasized that our awareness and understanding of the history of these ceremonies has been affected by oppression. Glen suggested that when British hierarchical systems were brought to North America, Aboriginal systems that were based on a holistic view were oppressed. One of the effects of this oppression was that Aboriginal people lost touch with the many metaphysical understandings and practices they once commonly held. Bernie noted that Christian beliefs were imposed upon Aboriginal people and that our own belief system was invalidated. As a result we were disempowered. She stated:

> I've talked [earlier] about people who have Christian beliefs and how they have been disempowered because they're Aboriginal people. And I think participating in sharing circles gives them a sense of, "gee, yea, we really did have our belief systems. They were really valid." I think it gives them a sense of pride that they have a heritage and prior to colonization we, Aboriginal people, had our own ways of doing things.

In several of the sharing circles in which I participated there were discussions of the importance of Aboriginal ceremonies, including sharing circles, to the well-being of Aboriginal people. The Elders in these circles often spoke of their gratefulness that these ceremonies continue despite the historical oppression and persecution that Aboriginal people faced when utilizing them. The Elders also emphasized the need for Aboriginal people to know and understand this history, so that we could then stand up for and maintain these ceremonies.

THE PHYSICAL ASPECT OF SHARING CIRCLES

While Glen noted that every sharing circle is unique and that he has supported participants in establishing their own circle process, there are several common attributes of sharing circles. These include common descriptive features of and specific attributes associated with the conductor, the participants and the process. These attributes and features were all associated with the implementation of sharing circles.

One of the features is the size the of the circles, which varies, but they are generally small (Hart 1996; Scott 1990). It is suggested that group sizes of ten to fifteen are often optimum (Guidelines for Talking Circles 1990). While Bernie acknowledged that she didn't "think there's a limit" to the number of participants in a sharing circle, Glen, Mary, Bernie and Fanny suggested that a circle can be too large if there are more than twenty participants. They stated that when a group is too large, people are less comfortable and less willing to share. Mary and Fanny suggested that up to fifteen people would be best. Glen identified a smaller group as being preferable. Smaller circles are preferred because people are more willing to trust one another (Bernie), to talk (Mary) and to open up (Glen). The participants also have more time and space to talk (Fanny). In the sharing circles in which I participated the number of participants varied from only five participants to over sixty, but most had between ten and twenty.

Circle size does affect the degree of sharing, with people generally being more willing to share their thoughts, feelings and experiences when the circles were smaller. However, in the circle that had over sixty people, I noted that many of the participants still had a significant willingness to share. It is important to note that in that situation almost all of the people were relatively well known to one another.

Another common feature of sharing circles is the length of the process. Usually, there is no time pressure for participants to contribute since they are allowed to speak freely without interruption, and they are aware that the circle may take an extended period of time to be completed (Guidelines for Talking Circles 1990). In my sharing circle experiences, I did not note any time restrictions. In the circle with over sixty participants, the first person started sharing at approximately 3:15 p.m. and the last person finished speaking at approximately 7:45 p.m. In another circle of five participants the total process lasted less than twenty minutes. Another sharing process lasted two days. In this case, the circle stopped for lunch and for the evening. It resumed the next day, and there was a break for lunch again. Usually, I did not feel that the amount of time for a circle to be completed limited the effectiveness of the circle. The most common exception was when both the amount of time and the number of participants were large. But, in these instances, I noted that people had not followed the guidelines previously identified by the conductor.

Bernie confirmed this point about time restrictions:

I don't think there's a limit. Usually a sharing circle takes as long as it needs to. I've heard of them taking days to finish. I've never participated in one that's that long, but when we were doing them we would give as much time as we needed. So if there were other things planned and we were still in the sharing circle … it was accepted and respected that we weren't finished yet. Sometimes it would go into the afternoon hours where there were other things planned. This took precedence over whatever else was planned because it was given enough time to finish.

Fanny noted that each person does not face a time restriction either: "Everybody has a chance to speak. And people, I think, can take as long as they want to speak." However, when circles become too large, some people get a feeling that people cannot share as extensively as they would like. Mary said "If there's too many people then the people in there won't be able to have the time to say too much. Like when I've been in a large circle, I don't want to say too much because there's too many people and they want the other people to get a chance to speak."

Sharing circles took place in a variety of locations. These locations included the outdoors, traditional camps, an office, a community conference room, a ceremonial lodge, teepees, people's homes, a church basement hall, a treatment centre and a classroom. The primary consideration for establishing a place appeared to be whether the site could accommodate the number of people attending. Bernie said that sharing circles can be conducted anywhere, "as long as there's enough room so that people can be comfortable, not lying around but at least being able to sit comfortably." An additional criteria was identified by Fanny: "I think it's important to go some place that's quiet. So that everything, literally speaking, can be heard. So it needs to be in a place that the quietest person, or the person with the lowest voice can be heard." It also had to accommodate the ceremonies that were conducted along with the sharing circles. Usually this accommodation related to whether smoke detectors would be set off by the smudging and pipe ceremonies.

Seating arrangements vary somewhat. In my experience, the participants were encouraged to sit in the circle so that they were not sitting behind one another. In most instances, if there were any gaps between individuals they were closed by the people moving to sit side by side. In one circle, an Elder told us that it was important to close these gaps so that people would be brought closer together and unified as one. In another instance, a gap in the circle was purposefully made to face the eastern direction to represent the place of beginnings. Another time, the room was too small for the number of people and some participants were forced to sit behind others. Overall, people generally sat wherever they preferred as long as it was within the circle.

Similarly, each conductor noted that people sit in a circle facing one another. Fanny stated that "people usually sit wherever they would like to sit" within the circle. She also suggested that if there were a large number of people then the circle "can be layered, like a ripple effect. There can be one circle, another circle behind them, and then another circle after that."

The Participants

People come to sharing circles through various means. For each of the sharing circles that I participated in, I was either informed through word of mouth, was invited or was a participant of another activity which included a sharing circle. Mary also noted that people are generally informed about sharing circles through word of mouth or they are invited. Bernie noted that in the particular sharing circles she has conducted, the participants were already involved in a treatment process that included these sharing circles.

My participation in the sharing circles was entirely voluntary. Once I was part of a circle, I did not feel coerced to participate more than I wanted. However, I did recognize that there is a strong group presence since most, if not all, of the participants followed the same systematic routine of sharing. I thought at the time that this presence could cause someone to feel pressured to participate more than they wanted to. In two of the sharing circles, there was at least one person who did not smudge. In seven sharing circles, there was at least one person who decided not to speak. Yet, despite the group presence of sharing circles, I did not note anyone specifically pressuring these people to smudge or to speak (see also Hart 1996; Scott 1991; Stevenson 1999).

The conductors I talked with stated that sharing circles are voluntary. Glen and Marg noted that it is helpful to accept that some people in the circle do not want to participate by sharing or smudging. Each person has the choice. Glen emphasized that the participants are responsible for their choices. He also highlighted that if people decided not to speak, they were still participating:

> Some people will take risks. Some people will sit back and listen. Through all of that, they're all learning. It's important that they keep their minds and their hearts open to the learning process. If

they choose to sit and watch, that's fine. They're still taking in the information. They're still seeing, still feeling, respecting that space. They're still learning anyway.

While in a circle, all efforts are to be made by all participants to remain until everyone has had the chance to express themselves (Hart 1996; Scott 1991). Indeed, it has been suggested that a basic rule of sharing circles is that "the group sits in a circle and each person gets a chance to say whatever is on their mind without being criticized or judged by others" (Guidelines for Talking Circles 1990:12). However, Bernie noted that at times there were people who had quit participating by leaving the circle before it was over, thus breaking the circle. She would get these individuals and bring them back to the circle:

> so a lot of times women, not understanding the sacredness of not breaking the circle, would walk out of the room because they were feeling so much pain or intense feeling. So what would happen usually is, if I was the facilitator, I would say, "I have to leave the circle for a minute." And go and try and get her so that she could come back into the circle. So in that way, towards the end, people had been there for a certain amount of time and then understood that you don't break the circle and that you don't leave the circle until it's over. But initially there were times when we had to, you know, leave to get somebody and bring them back.

Related to participation is acceptance. I noticed that almost anyone who wanted to participate in a sharing circle was accepted. While rare, sometimes people were turned away from the circle for very specific reasons. I observed one such instance. An individual who wanted to participated was so intoxicated that he was staggering and his speech was loud and slurred. In this situation the conductor told the individual that he was welcome at a time when he was sober and able to fully participate without disruption.

Fanny, Bernie and Mary noted that, generally, people are not excluded from participating in a sharing circle. Fanny also highlighted that interested people are not turned away as long as they followed particular guidelines:

> Everybody's welcome. I've even seen people who've been drunk, under the influence of alcohol, and they will come to the circle. So

nobody's turned away. I guess it depends on the intent of the circle. But there's ways of behaving at a sharing circle. I don't think I've seen anybody turned away when people behave and follow the rules.

Overall, the importance of accepting all people and whatever degree of participation they want to give, including not participating, has been emphasized. This is balanced with respecting the circle processes, such as not breaking the circle by leaving.

As noted previously by Fanny, some circles have particular intentions, and these circles can have participation limited to only certain people. In one circle in which I participated, the circle was open only to the first twelve people who confirmed that they were going to attend. Fanny, Mary and Bernie also told me that there are times when circles are open only to particular people. For example, Bernie noted that she had conducted circles that were only for women who had been battered.

Another factor that influenced participation was when a woman was on her time. Bernie identified women's time as when women were "menstruating, their cycle." It has been noted that a woman's time is spiritually significant and important within Aboriginal traditions (Anderson 2000; Stevenson 1999). It is viewed as a time when a woman's power is heightened and when women are already in a natural ceremony which requires their full participation. Thus, the degree and manner of their participation in circles will be different, depending upon the women, Elders, conductors and medicine bundles present for the sharing circle.

Conductors of the sharing circles in which I participated supported women on their time in different ways. In one sharing circle, the conductor stated prior to it beginning that women on their time should leave the room. In two other circles, the conductors stated that women on their time had to sit outside the circle. One of these conductors still had the women share from outside the circle, while the other conductor did not have the women share. In other circles there was no mention of women being on their time. Significant to note was that the times when women were requested not to be present were the times when medicine bundles—the bundles which the conductors used to carry their sacred objects and plant medicines—were present and to be used.

Marg said:

> There's a high level of respect for women on their time. I feel when I was in my early stage of learning that wasn't my place to be

because it created a disharmony in my life. My emotions, quite often, were very high and I didn't need extra people to be breathing down my neck with their problems when I was struggling to deal with my own issues. So, it's to be considerate for women on their time. And if they're not aware of it, just mention it to them because that's a form of learning, eh? It's time for them to take care of themselves.

Bernie also discussed women on their time. However, she outlined how women were able to participate in the sharing circle while they were on their time:

> Once all the women were in, we would start like a smudge. We used sage because, depending on what plant you picked, women can use it at any time. So it didn't matter if they were on their time, they could still use the smudge. There's a female plant and a male plant that you can pick. So as long as you picked the female plant you could use it for women who were on their time. So it, the smudge, didn't exclude anybody that way. If somebody was on their time, they could still come into the sharing circle.

Participants shared particular responsibilities. This was evident in the sharing circles in which I participated and in the statements made by the five conductors who spoke with me. The first responsibility that most conductors emphasized was respectfulness. During my participation in circles respect was identified as meaning paying attention to the speakers without interruption and offering prayers for the speakers. In general, this means respecting what people say, what their views are, and how they are able to express themselves (see Regnier 1995; Katz and St. Denis 1991)

Mary identified "respecting everybody" as one of the basic rules of sharing circles. Fanny connected respect to the participants being equal: "Everybody has a right to be heard. Everybody has a right to speak since nobody's better than anybody else. Everybody that comes there is very important and everybody, each person, deserves to be respected." She also emphasized that "the sharing circle is only as strong as those who sit down and show respect." Bernie spoke repeatedly about respect. She extended the concept of respect to mean the validating of people's feelings, thoughts and experiences by paying attention to the person and not pressuring anyone to finish speaking. Circle participants must respect the privacy of others as well as the wisdom of the council or circle as a whole (Bopp et al. 1985). Marg, Glen and Bernie associated respect with non-interference, even when a participant disagreed with what was being said. For example, Marg stated:

> If you have a disagreement with the person that's conducting the sharing circle, or if you do not really like what that person is saying at that time, you did not have the right to interfere and say, "well I don't like what you're saying" or "how dare you say this" because that was not acceptable.

Very important to respect is the maintenance of confidentiality. According to many Elders, what is said in the circle is to remain in the circle. Ultimately, respects means "healing begins when we reach down into ourselves and understand the narrowness of our own perspectives and lives, show respect for another way of life, and are willing to learn from it" (Peat 1994: 152).

The second responsibility highly emphasized was patient listening. In almost every circle that I participated in, with only one exception, the conductors emphasized that when another participant speaks, we are to listen. Fanny also stressed that "listening is very important. Listening is highly, highly active and that we're to listen with big, open hearts, with an open mind, and to try to take in as much as you can. I try to listen from where that person is speaking from." Glen noted that people need "to listen to that other person. Truly listen. Not just go, hmm, yea, hmm, uh huh, uh huh, yea, and act like they're listening, but to truly listen from the heart." People are to do more than just hear the words. They are encouraged to listen so that they can understand the world through the speaker's eyes and contribute to solutions (Morrissette et al. 1993). Bopp et al. (1985: 76) suggests that people are expected to "listen with courtesy to what others say, even if you feel that what they are saying is worthless. Listen with your heart." Listening also means that people are not to interrupt the speaker with their own thoughts or ideas (Clarkson et al. 1992; Janzen et al. 1994; Morrissette et al. 1993). Participants are not to focus their thoughts only on what they are going to say when their turn comes but are also encouraged to pray silently for the one who is speaking (Guidelines for Talking Circles 1990). Over time, participants come to understand they are required to exercise patience and listen in ways that are non-judgemental and without condemnation or ridicule (Guidelines for Talking Circles 1990; Regnier 1994; Stevenson 1999). If there is to be any judging, then it is self-judgement that is used to develop self-determination (Regnier 1994).

Glen and Fanny connected listening with respect. Glen identified that when one person was speaking, "the other participants or people sitting are respectful and listen." He explained further that people in sharing circles "respect individuals for who they are as human beings and allow them the right to voice their own opinion. They give them the respect of listening, truly listening to what they have to say." Fanny also noted this connection between respect and listening: "One way of showing respect is by listening to whoever is speaking. Not to say anything but to listen."

Sharing was a third responsibility identified. Indeed, sharing is encouraged for the wellness of the individual and of the group. Sharing may involve people expressing themselves in any manner that is comfortable, including through personal stories, examples, metaphors or analytical statements (Guidelines for Talking Circles 1991). Modig (cited in Scott 1991) explained that her sharing involves speaking about her innermost feelings. While sharing may involve speaking about personal experiences within the circle, it may also involve other means of contributing. Indeed, being present in the circle and providing attentive support are considered forms of sharing (Guidelines for Talking Circles 1990; Stevenson 1999). Each participant makes the personal choice as to the depth and level of sharing with which they feel most comfortable (Antone and Hill 1990).

Two additional responsibilities were highlighted. Fanny suggested that participants need to bring supportive attitudes to the circle: "What makes it special is the attitude they have when they come." She also strongly emphasized the humbleness that she had felt in sharing circles, indicating that people need to present themselves as being no more special than others. Participants are encouraged to focus their thoughts and comments positively and avoid putting anyone down, including themselves (Hart 1996). Indeed, participants are being prepared to be co-counsellors. Antone and Hill (1990) define co-counselling as listening, paying attention and supporting individuals with kindness and warmth while they release any kind of distress. Participants also provide one another with mutual support for the healing and growth processes (Antone and Hill 1990; Regnier 1995). This is tied to another responsibility people have when it is not their turn to speak. According to Bernie, "People are asked to pray during that time so that they can not only get their own thoughts together but help whoever is talking to be able to express what they're thinking and feeling and what life is like for them."

The Conductor

Sharing circles usually have experienced conductors, sometimes referred to as facilitators or leaders (Hart 1996; Guidelines for Talking Circles 1990). Fanny emphasized that the "leader has a huge role" and that the strength of a sharing circle depends significantly upon the conductor. She suggested that the conductor must be kind, gentle, respectful, moral, ethical, confident, strong and flexible. Mary said that the conductor should be a good listener and be patient and accommodating. Glen emphasized that conductors should be accepting, while Bernie emphasized that they should be respectful of the participants. Also, conductors are to be non-judgemental, acknowledge contributions and when necessary clarify comments. They must be prepared to implement some basic counselling techniques, such as empathy and non-verbal encouragement (Guidelines for Talking Circles, 1990).

In most of the sharing circles in which I participated, it seemed to me that the conductors could be characterized as having these attributes. For example, in one sharing circle, it was clear that the conductor had an established process for conducting circles. He completed each task with assurance and remained respectful of each participant by listening intently to each of them without interruption. When one participant became silent for an extended period of time, the conductor remained patient and waited for the individual to complete her turn. When another participant expressed significant grief, he demonstrated through his facial expressions that he was empathizing with the person. In a different circle, the conductor was faced with a youth who was so impressed at holding the attention of several adults that he did not want to relinquish his turn. In this case, the conductor waited for the youth to end his turn at his own pace. He did not reprimand the youth at any point as if he was holding up the process. Another conductor demonstrated her gentleness and firmness through her manner. When she spoke her voice was soft and soothing, yet when she outlined the guidelines she appeared to be clear, consistent and firm.

There are exceptions, of course, however few in number. I was in only one sharing circle where the conductor did not demonstrate patience and respect. This conductor would interrupt the person speaking and give her own impressions of what was being said. She also demonstrated impatience through her body language and heavy loud sighs when someone else was speaking.

Conductors of sharing circles have certain responsibilities. The first responsibility of conductors of sharing circles is to prepare themselves:

There's a process for going into each circle, whether it's a healing circle, sharing circle or teaching circle. You need to prepare yourself. Facilitators need to prepare themselves. There are different ways of preparing. I think some people will smoke tobacco, and many people will smudge, pray, and … really slow down. And I think you then have to really tune into yourself and try to remind yourself to listen. (Fanny)

Similarly, in most of my experiences, the first thing each of the conductors did was arrange the smudge and opening prayer. The conductors assigned helpers to smudge everyone in the circle and either said the prayer or requested that a participant—an Elder if present—say the prayer. Bernie also discussed the inclusion of a prayer: "Usually the facilitator said a prayer to start the circle or you could ask one of the participants to do it."

In initiating the circle, the conductor outlines the process to be followed in the circle (Hart 1996). They often emphasize the importance of listening to one another, of not interrupting others when they speak, of respecting what others are sharing and of maintaining confidentiality. For example, one conductor reminded all the participants that what is said in the circle was to remain in the circle, that we should only tell others outside this circle about what we have shared and not what other people have shared. Another conductor told us that if we took anything from the circle, we must use it only in a good way that does not bring harm to anyone. It was often stated that people were not required to talk if they did want to talk and that when their turn came they could just pass their turn to the next person.

I noticed that in each of the sharing circles, with exception of two, the conductors gave quite precise guidelines for the circle. They did not consume a lot of time outlining the guidelines and process; nor did any of them spend much time confirming that everyone understood the guidelines. In one of the two exceptions the conductor did not spend any time going over the guidelines. However, in this circle the people had regularly participated in circles with one another. In the other situation, the conductor was not precise in outlining the guidelines. She also spent a lot of time, in comparison to the other conductors, asking the participants if each guideline she attempted to explain was "okay."

Glen also noted, "One of the first things that I do is go through some basic rules or responsibilities that each of the participants should consider before we actually move into anything. The purpose of the sharing circle is something that I establish first." Mary identified that she "makes right in that sharing circle" by explaining the circle process. She tells "them some of the rules, like about confidentiality, respect and talking only when it's your turn." She also explains that the participants are to be respectful: "You don't comment on somebody else or take it personally." Bernie focused on the need for a conductor to tell people who have never participated in a sharing circle about the process and guidelines:

> When you get somebody new, you tell them about respect. You tell them that a sharing circle is there for people to be able to express how they're feeling, what they're thinking, and who they are, without feeling like they're going to be challenged or that somebody is going to take offence to what they say. And that you need to be respectful, even if you disagree with somebody in the sharing circle. The respect for people to be able to say what they feel and what they think is very much a part of the sharing circle.

Only some conductors prefer that circles remain unbroken. Four of the conductors of the circles in which I participated said they preferred that once the circle had started people should not break the circle by leaving unless they absolutely had to. Another conductor outlined this condition prior to the smudging and prayer so that the people could make the decision of whether to participate or not. Only Bernie identified that the circle should not be broken. Marg, Mary, Fanny and Glen did not insist on this condition.

Once the process and guidelines were outlined, conductors would direct the sharing process to begin. During the sharing period, conductors were very supportive as evidenced by their body language and their focused attention on the speakers. When a speaker was finished they would not comment, but they would acknowledge the speaker verbally by such sayings as "hi hi" or "ah ho."

When others in the circle were not paying attention to the speaker and were disruptive, conductors usually stared at these people to get their attention so that the conductor's disapproval was seen. When conductors addressed the circle in this indirect manner, the disruptive person quit being disruptive. In a few situations, I noted that conductors had to interrupt the circle when a speaker was finished in order to remind the participants generally about the importance of listening and respect. I did not note a conductor in any of the circles specifically address a particular person for being disruptive.

To be sure, there are some exceptions. Of the twelve circles that I reflected upon, there was only one exception to these dynamics of the conductor. In one particular circle the conductor herself was disruptive, occasionally speaking to the persons beside her when others were taking their turn. When others in this circle were disruptive she did not attempt to address their behaviour.

After everyone has shared, including the conductors, the circle is almost always brought to a close by a closing prayer given by the conductor or a participant. The final acknowledgements, either handshakes and/or hugs between the participants, are then initiated by the conductors. Bernie and Fanny acknowledged that once everyone had the opportunity to share, the conductor would close the circle with a prayer. For example, Bernie stated, "After everybody had shared, the closing of the sharing was the saying of a prayer." They also noted that the conductor would close the circle by having each participant shake hands or hug the other participants.

Throughout the whole process, one of the main responsibilities of the conductor was to create a safe environment for the participants (Glen, Mary, Bernie and Fanny). Bernie frequently focused on the importance of creating a trusting and safe environment:

> [Sharing circles are] a way of helping people to feel safe and to trust what they're feeling and their opinions. They are able to share with people in a safe, trusting way. To me that's the most important thing. I think that sharing circles allow people to really express who they are and what they're feeling. They can say what they think and without feeling like somehow somebody's going to take offence to what they say or somebody's going to challenge how they're feeling. I think it's a way of validating people's thoughts and feelings about whatever's happening to them.

She stated that, in order to ensure a safe place, the conductor should:

> make sure that everybody has time to say what they need to say. Again the conductor should also keep the circle moving, to monitor whether people are reacting or challenging other people, and to, I hesitate to say, referee. When people make a comment about somebody else, or what somebody else has said, the conductor needs to make sure that people are aware that they are there for themselves and whatever somebody else says is that person's. So, that's the basic job of running it and to make sure people are respectful of each other.

Of course, respectfulness is an essential ingredient that enables people to feel safe. As Bernie put it:

> I think that one of the jobs of facilitating the sharing circle is to help people deal with their own self rather than reacting to somebody else. I think you have to be very careful with it. I don't think you talk. You wait until the person is finished. Then, if you want to say something at the end of their talk, you don't specifically point them out, but you say something like, "I really encourage people to talk about what they're feeling rather than reacting to somebody else's stuff." So you may interject after people have finished talking but you never outright challenge somebody in the middle of their sharing. Again, that's part of the way you show respect.

At times, Elders or traditional healers are asked by conductors to be involved in sharing circles (Hart 1996; Stevenson 1999). In these circumstances, the conductor may ask the guest to direct or make specific contributions to the process, for example, opening and closing the circle with a prayer, bringing sacred objects to guide the process, and/or conducting other ceremonies, such as a pipe ceremony, within the circle (Hart 1996: Regnier 1995). The Elder or healer may also contribute to the circle by providing teachings and/or answers to specific questions (Stiegelbauer 1996).

Sharing Circle Processes
Processes for conducting circles have been acknowledged for activities such as sentencing circles (Hollow Water Community Holistic Circle Healing 1993), story circles (Regnier 1995) and check-ins prior to meetings (Ross 1996). A process for sharing circles might be as follows:

> Participants are seated in a circle facing towards the centre. There should be no gaps as all are seated side by side. Once the process begins, the circle should not be broken by individuals leaving during the process. There is usually a facilitator who leads the sharing circle. This individual outlines the process to the group. Upon completing this task, the facilitator has the individual on the immediate left begin the discussion. The format allows individuals to focus on a predetermined topic, or to be free to share their thoughts on any topic they wish. The first person may speak

for any length of time, or not at all. Others in the group cannot interrupt the individual who is sharing.... Once the individual has spoken, the person to the immediate left takes the role of speaker. This individual is given the same opportunities as the first person.... The process continues until all people within the circle have shared. (Hart 1996: 67)

There was a general process followed in most of the sharing circles in which I participated, one similar to the process followed by the conductors I talked to. They identified that sharing circles often start with a smudging ceremony (also see Hart 1996; Hollow Water Community Holistic Circle Healing 1993; Scott 1991). Smudging is seen as a spiritual act which works to take out the negative energy in the room, in the participants and in the process (Stevenson 1999). Smudge is made out of sacred medicines, such as sweetgrass, cedar, sage and/or tobacco, and is burned, with the smoke being used to cleanse oneself (Bernie, Marg, Mary, Fanny). Bernie explained that the way to smudge "is the same way people wash their bodies.... It's very much like a washing motion. So you smudge all over. As they wash they ask for guidance for that day." She said smudging cleanses your spiritual self and gets rid of negative feelings so that the participants can share whatever goes on in their lives.

Marg noted that smudging "opens your mind," so that people are in the circle with a "positive mind." Mary added that smudging not only cleans the person but also the physical environment: "It cleans you out and opens you. It clears out the area where you're at in case there's some negative energy." Bernie suggested that smudging also helps people to focus on their own growth and what they are doing to help that growth.

Fanny noted that circles can sometimes use smudges at the end. In one instance, she asked an Elder, who had just finished conducting a sharing circle, if they could smudge at that time. Her request was based upon the need to get rid of burdens they were carrying after the circle. In this situation, she felt that the smudging helped them to unload the burdens so that they did not leave with the heaviness.

As suggested earlier, circle participants are not forced to take part in the smudge. Bernie said people were allowed to pass over this part of the sharing circle:

So anybody that came in after that [the smudge], one of the other participants would go over why we used the sharing circle and why we smudged. People were never forced, if they didn't understand why we smudged or if they chose not to be a part of the smudge, they could leave and then come back once the sharing circle started.

Glen noted another way in which people who did not participate in smudging could remain part of the sharing circle:

> Let's say you have a particular circle where ninety-nine percent of the people want a smudge and one person doesn't. Well, I will just have them step back when the smudge bowl comes around. You know they have that space, that respect where they don't have to if they didn't want to.

In my experiences of sharing circles, not only would the smudging occur at the beginning of the circle, but once everyone had the opportunity to smudge, the bowl or shell which contained the smudging medicines was placed in the centre of the circle. This same placement of the smudge bowl is followed by Bernie, Fanny, Marg, Mary and Glen.

In addition, I observed other items being placed in the centre of the circle. For example, one conductor placed a medicine bundle, candle, water, rattles, a drum and some personal sacred items in the centre. These items were arranged in a particular manner and referred to as the central altar. Alternately, another sharing circle occurred around a bonfire. At this circle, wood for the fire, tea and water for drinking, and the smudge bowl were placed within the circle. Glen, Fanny, Marg and Mary noted that there may be a medicine bundle in the middle of the circle. Fanny often "put in the centre … a blanket … a symbolic blanket … a little one." Bernie focused upon the inclusion of water:

> The smudge would be placed in the middle along with either a bowl of water, or a cup of water, or something. And again, it would allow people to focus. The water was also symbolic of life. Water is life giving. It can also be very restful for people, so if they didn't have a rock then they can focus on the water and just remain focused.

Finally, Mary noted that when sharing circles occur in a teepee there usually is a bonfire in the centre of the circle.

The next step that usually occurred in the sharing circles in which I participated was an opening prayer. Fanny stressed that prayer is very important and that it is one of the key elements that makes sharing circles so powerful. The prayer is said by the conductor, an Elder in the circle or by someone in the circle who is invited to do so by the conductor. Glen was the only conductor that I talked with who did not directly say that sharing circles would include an opening prayer. Bernie noted that, while the conductor usually said the prayer, the conductor may request someone in the circle to say an opening prayer. Fanny identified that the conductor may request that an Elder say the opening prayer.

In most of the sharing circles in which I participated, once the smudging and opening prayer were completed, the conductors outlined what process would be followed and the guidelines. In matching the variety of processes that can be followed, there are various guidelines to support sharing circles. Most of these guidelines are similar. Antone and Hill (1990: 9), for example, suggest for the healing circle process, that the conductor tell the participants:

1. You belong here just because you are here and for no other reason.
2. What is true for you will be determined by what is within you, by what you directly feel and by what you find making sense within you. The way in which you live inside yourself is important.
3. Our first purpose is to make contact with each other.
4. We will try to be as honest as possible in expressing who we really are and what we really feel. We will attempt to express as much as we can.
5. We will listen to the person inside of each of us, and we will take ownership of our feelings.
6. We will respect and listen to everyone.
7. Everything discussed in the circle is real, and we do not pretend that it isn't.
8. Any decisions made within the circle need everyone to take part in some way.
9. I am responsible for protecting each member's place within the circle.
10. I will ensure that everyone in the circle is provided with the opportunity to speak and will ensure that you are heard.

These guidelines are a way of building trust within the circle.

After these steps, the conductors begin the sharing process by giving the person to the left of them the first opportunity to speak. While the discussion can focus on a predetermined topic, generally the focus includes comments on whatever the participants desire to share (Hart 1996). After the first person has spoken, the person on the left of the first speaker is given the opportunity to speak. The process is repeated in this manner so that each person has an opportunity to speak, including the conductor. This process symbolically follows the patterns seen in the universe, such as the direction of the sun. In every case, the conductors also participate by sharing about personal matters. In this manner the conductors are also full participants.

Bernie, Fanny, Mary and Marg each noted a similar process of the participants taking turns to speak by passing to the left, that is, going clockwise. While Glen noted this process of moving to the left, he also stated that he did not know why the people would "automatically go to the left," other than that being a subconscious or unconscious thing. He added:

> You know, people will automatically go to the left when they're done. And, then just to throw people off, sometimes they'll say "let's go to the right." And you know, probably people over here will be squirming, you know, like "guys, they're going the wrong way." You know. But I do that just for the heck of it. And to me there's nothing major about going to the right.

However, Fanny stated her concern that changing the direction of the sharing process makes the process a little confusing. Marg was even more concerned about which way the process moved. Her explanation for moving clockwise was that the circle process follows patterns found in the world, particularly the sun, in order to maintain harmony.

On a point about variations in the sharing process, Bernie outlined how a sharing circle can be ongoing over an extended period of time for a particular group of people. She described one particular circle: "So when we first started a group, we usually had an intake in September, we would start the circles. So we had people that were there for at least three months at a time within the circle so they got really connected. And then any time we had a bunch of new people we would start another circle." The same process was followed at each re-meeting of the circle. In my participation, the closest I came to an ongoing circle was when one circle continued over two days.

An additional variation in sharing circle processes is that they may include more than a single round of sharing (Scott 1990). Fanny noted this variation and identified it as a guided circle:

> Also, there may be more than one round. The first round may be

people just introducing themselves. I guess that's the process of opening up the circle. So for me what I like is for people to introduce themselves, a chance to introduce themselves, and share whatever they'd like to share about themselves. Some people will state why they're there. Then you can do a round and people will share. And then you can do another round so you can do a number of rounds. And it seems my experience is that with each round it seems that we can go deeper into our sharing.

The people I talked with all spoke of the conductor fully participating in the sharing. Bernie discussed her participation as a conductor most directly: "The facilitator needs to be part of the group. They're no different."

In six circles that I participated in, the process of taking turns to speak was guided with an object, either an eagle feather or a rock. When going over the guidelines and process, the conductors usually stated that whoever is holding the object is the designated speaker. In the sharing circles she had conducted, Mary would use a feather, rock or "whatever." Glen noted that sometimes a talking stick may be used. Bernie identified using only a rock in the sharing circles she had conducted. Fanny noted using a stone, a feather or a ribbon at times, while at other times she did not use anything. Bernie explained the reason she used a rock:

> The way the rock was used was when a person finished sharing they would pass the rock on to the next person. I think it helped them hang on to something. You know, it was something concrete that felt safe. Again, I think it's to do with safety and feeling comfortable that you have something in your hand. If you're nervous you can play with it. It allows you to remain connected with something.

She later added, "Part of the reason we used the rock was because you remain connected to something that comes from the earth." Fanny concurred:

> The eagle feather is also very strong and it gives people something to hold on to when they share. I think it's comforting to hold a symbol. It also provides some reassurance I think. I've seen people hold an eagle feather and stroke it and I've seen some people express their anger holding an eagle feather and really hit it hard,

smash, smash. And you know what, that eagle feather never breaks. I've never seen an eagle feather break no matter how many hands it has gone through. People stroke it, poke it and flick it back and forth. It never loses its shape. I'm always amazed with how these symbols are so very strong. Ribbons may be used and these symbols have been blessed too. People sometimes will remark on the stone that when the stone is being passed, it becomes energized. So people can feel the stone heat up because it's been passed from one person to another.

Through the passing of the object each person had an opportunity to speak. I noticed that speakers held the rock for various amounts of time. Some people held the object but did not speak. Still others just passed the rock on without speaking. During the time the object was held, the other participants were quiet and appeared to be listening to the speaker. Eventually the object returned back to the conductor, who then had an opportunity to speak.

Another alternative to going around in the circle (Guidelines for Talking Circles 1990; Hart 1996; Regnier 1994; Scott 1991) requires the use of an object, such as a rock, feather or talking stick. In this process, when an individual wishes to speak, they are required to be holding the object; otherwise they are to be listening to the speaker. When the speaker has finished they put the object down. Someone else may then pick it up and take a turn at speaking.

I have experienced a few circles where this sharing process was followed. In one particular group the people had been regularly participating in circles together, and the first opportunity to speak was left open to anyone. An object would be placed in the centre of the circle and anyone who wanted to pick it up would initiate the sharing process. When the person was finished, they would place the object back in the centre of the circle. People who had yet to share were then allowed to pick up the object. This process continued until each person who wanted to speak had picked up the object.

In another circle, a similar process was followed without the use of an object to act as a guide. In this instance, the conductor stated that we would not have to go around the circle in any particular manner. Anyone who wanted to talk could talk when they felt like it. As a result, people sitting across from or on either side of the last speaker would take their turn. At times two people would be speaking at the same moment, creating a haphazard process. Marg's comment about this type of sharing process is significant: "It goes in a circle. You cannot criss-cross. If you do that, then they [her grandparents and the people of that generation] believe that you created disharmony." Indeed it appeared to me that this circle had, at particular moments, a significant amount of disharmony and that it was associated directly with the non-circular process of sharing that was followed.

At the end of each of the sharing circles that I participated in which had an opening prayer, a closing prayer also occurred. Once again the conductor, a designated Elder or someone else from the circle said the closing prayer. Usually, if the conductor said the opening prayer, then the conductor also said the closing prayer. Similarly, the same Elder that opened the circle with a prayer usually said the closing prayer. However, when a participant from the circle was invited to say the opening prayer, another person was asked to say the closing prayer. In addition, all but one circle had some form of a hand shaking or hugging process where each person was given the opportunity to shake the hand or hug each of the other participants. The conductors would assign someone to begin the process, if they did not start it themselves. Bernie, Fanny, Marg and Mary stated that sharing circles usually include a closing prayer and acknowledgements such as handshakes or hugging. For example, Bernie stated, "At the end of the sharing circle they [the participants] would be hugging each other and leave feeling really good."

The atmosphere of the sharing circles that I participated must be highlighted as a reflection of the types of relationships present through the process. For the most part, in each of these sharing circles the atmosphere was one of mutuality and support. While everyone was encouraged to benefit from what was shared, they also were supported to share their own contributions through their presence, what they had to say and what they expressed emotionally. For example, in one sharing circle the conductor emphasized that we could all learn from one another since we all have a significant view of the things we had experienced. My feeling about this circle and most of the other circles was that my contributions were just as significant as those of the other participants. In several of my circle experiences, the conductors said that we were not forced or required to take all that is said by the participants. These conductors explained that we only had to take what we needed and perceived as good. Other aspects were to be left alone. These comments contributed to the calm, supportive sense of the circle since there were no pressures placed upon us.

I only experienced one exception to this atmosphere. In this circle the conductor was less clear in outlining the guidelines and process and was also disruptive. It seemed that the conductor deemed her views as being the most important. It was as if she took the role of an all-knowing expert. At one time, when she spoke to what had been said by a participant, I noticed the participant looking down and slightly shaking her head. It appeared to me that the participant was displeased that what she had said had, at least, been negated.

Glen discussed the importance of a cooperative atmosphere and the avoidance of hierarchy:

> You know, here we have a hierarchal system which to me comes from the Europeans that clashed with tribes and their philosophies that are in a cyclical system. Now if you look at it in terms of the circle, what are some of the benefits or positive aspects of the circle itself? Well, it creates an atmosphere of cooperation. It creates an atmosphere of equality. Look at just the symbol itself. You put people in a circle, everybody's the same. Now when you come from a hierarchal system where someone is at the front and someone is at the back, or at the top or the bottom, what does that induce? It creates competition. It creates this atmosphere of someone who is better than or someone who's less than. So there's a difference.

Bernie also noted the lack of hierarchy: "It's not hierarchal. It's not like I'm the teacher and I know everything. I'm there to learn as much as I'm sharing. I'm learning as much as I can from the stories that I hear." Both Fanny and Bernie suggested that the lack of hierarchy included the conductor as well. "Everybody in that circle is on the same plane. You know, there's no hierarchy in the sharing circle. Everybody is the same. Even the facilitator should blend into that" (Fanny). Bernie also noted that:

> The facilitator needs to be a part of the group. You're no different. You're there to help make sure that the circle keeps going but you also share. Again, it's part of that whole thing that I can share whatever I'm feeling as a facilitator, whatever things are happening in my life that I'm finding hard, or that I'm excited about, or that I'm happy about.

THE EMOTIONAL, MENTAL AND SPIRITUAL ASPECTS OF SHARING CIRCLES

Healing in Circles

Sharing circles can lead to various results, including emotional validation and healing. Antone and Hill (1990) identify four levels of circles which can have healing properties. Level one is the talking circle where people become aware of the original hurts. Level two is the sharing circle, where a high degree of trust is formed and individuals begin to express painful emotions. Level three is the healing circle, where people work through memories of painful experiences and develop trust in the intuitive and spiritual messages they receive. Level four is the spiritual circle, where individuals reclaim and strengthen their spiritual gifts and integrate cultural teachings and practices in their healing processes and lives. Regnier (1994: 140) suggests that "through the circle, [participants] can visualize themselves as whole persons, see connections between different aspects of their lives, and determine how to balance their development." Through this reflection and interpretation, they may participate in a healing process. Healing also occurs through the participant's expression of feelings that stem from painful experiences and through the attention given to the speaker by all the participants.

Glen identified that for his own healing process to begin he had to learn how to become aware of what he was feeling, especially since "most people are out of touch with their emotional, spiritual aspects." He further outlined that part of the healing process for people is for them to express their emotions and that sharing circles are "one way of learning those things. Expression of emotions. Expression of feelings." He shared a story of how important emotions are to sharing circles and healing:

> Well I remember, my example, in a circle and then one of the things I was processing was my relationship with my stepfather. We were never very close. He was an alcoholic, a raging alcoholic, and there was really no bonding that took place in my relationship with him. So I needed to work on my resentment and my anger and rage towards him so one of the things that I was asked to do was pick someone in the group who resembled him and then I was to face this person and express what I was feeling. Well, I'm bawling and snot and everything is running down my nose. And so the facilitator asked R. to go and get a Kleenex, "get G a Kleenex." So I'm processing my stuff with the guy. And then R.

comes back with one ply of Kleenex [chuckle] sticks it in our face, and we look at each other and we look at back and we just all bust out laughing. The laughter was so good to us. Even the rest of the group. They were getting caught up in my work. They were starting to connect and starting to cry and when that happened. Boom, split, we flew back the other way and we were all laughing at my situation. I don't know if R. meant to do that, I'll never know, you know, because he's in another place now. At that time it was perfect. You know, the laughter is important. It's got to be part of this. And I see a lot of that in other communities that work together. Laughter brings people together. So, with tears, there has to be the other side of that, eh.

Bernie made a similar suggestion. For her, sharing circles, as a helping method, are really valuable because they help break down taboos against talking about painful emotional experiences:

> Initially I think people felt, they only shared superficial things within the circle, expressed really limited things, "I'm feeling really bad today," or "but I'll get over it." As time progressed and as they got more trusting with each other, they would share more about, "I'm remembering something today and I'm feeling really bad." And people would feel comfortable with crying and sharing emotions within the circle.

Mary outlined that a sharing circle "helps you to cry or even laugh ... helps you express emotions." Fanny also acknowledged that people express emotions in sharing circles, including hurt, pain, frustration and anger. She also highlighted that when people share their stories they may trigger other people's memories. In this way they may feel certain emotions even when they are not speaking about their own lives:

> I think when you go to a sharing circle and you're listening, you will see yourself in what is being said. Often you will see yourself. That's why you learn at sharing circles. You'll see yourself, you'll see your whole life. You'll see what happened when you were a child. You'll see what happened as you were growing up. You'll see your mom. You'll see your dad, your grandma and your grandpa, your neighbours, your brothers and sisters. So whatever is being said you may have lived that already or may trigger off some

memory.... And you'll feel. So if someone is expressing fear, you know, in meeting an animal in the bush for example, you'll feel that too. Or if there is happiness or sadness, you'll probably feel that too.

In each of the sharing circles that I participated in, there was at least one person, but usually more, who intensely expressed emotions of sadness, anger, frustration, joy or fear. These emotions were expressed through various methods, such as crying, raised voices, laughter and nervousness. I also personally experienced a variety of intense emotions when listening and when I shared in circles. For example, I recall one circle where I was feeling very confused. I watched as each person shared. Most of them hung their heads down, and in a sad sounding monotone, stated that they were very happy to be there. Yet, it seemed as if I was feeling personal pain and grief that was coming from many of them. When it came time for me to share, I presented how confused I felt. I shared that I was experiencing their pain and grief. I had tears in my eyes and had a difficult time speaking. One of the two Elders who were conducting the circle watched me closely. When I finished speaking, he interjected in the circle process and stated that he felt these emotions as well and that he would have cried with me if I had started to cry openly.

The healing aspect of sharing circles can go beyond emotional expression. It can carry further into releasing long held feelings that are affecting the wellness of people. Glen suggested that it was through this emotional expression in sharing circles that he was able to "discharge the stuff, this turmoil" and "cleanse and purify myself." Fanny also noted the discharging, or letting go of, particular feelings. She said that "sometimes maybe there is resentment or anger or fear or something that I want to let go. I think a sharing circle is a good place to let it go," and that circles are "a place where a great emotion can be left." Marg associated the discharging as being similar to seeing a counsellor and letting go of baggage:

> You use sharing circles when quite often you'd go see a counsellor. You know, in this society we go see the counsellor. But in our sharing circle we go within our own people. And we talk about the dysfunction or the hardships that we are encountering and once we've dealt with them we feel a lot better because we no longer need to carry that extra baggage of problems. You've dealt with it and it's gone. You may not come full terms to resolving the issue or the problem but at least you're able to voice what's bothering you.

Similarly, Bernie suggested that sharing circles could be used as a treatment method. Mary noted that even if people are unable to talk about what they are facing so that they may express their emotions or let go of their emotions, they are still able to receive help in other ways. She explained:

> When somebody's talking and if you're unable to talk [because] you're shy when another person talks about something … you're able to relate so in that way you don't have to say it. Its like it gets said for you so in that way you're helping yourself or that person's helping you just by telling their story if you're unable to do it. And, also when somebody's talking about something really painful that you went through, it also helps you because it allows you to cry or even laugh with the others.

Bernie also noted this mutual support and validation of feelings through the sharing of similar stories:

> I really think … the sharing circle is most effective when a group of people who have had similar experiences can really share. Can really feel an inclusion within a group, to say, "yea, I went through that too" you know, "I can really empathize with whatever" you know "I can really understand how you're feeling." Because they then are not alone.

Ross (1996: 152–53) notes how such sharing may result in the normalizing of people's feelings:

> When they come into the circles, however, they listen as team members tell their own stories, revealing the rage they felt. Each of those stories then serves to validate all of those feelings, in the sense of saying, "yes, we know those feelings, they are *normal* feelings in this situation, there is nothing wrong or disturbing about you."

In all but one of the circles in which I participated there were people who expressed, either at the end of their turn to speak or after the circle had finished, that they felt "better," "lighter," or "relieved." At the time of one particular sharing circle, I was feeling overwhelmed with what I was facing in my personal life. During my turn, I outlined how I felt angry, fearful and sad and how these feelings were tied to events that had occurred long ago. I felt comfortable enough to cry, which I did. When my turn was over, I felt that I had been heard and supported. More significantly, I felt some relief even though I knew that what I was facing was not gone. I believe that I was able to discharge some of my turmoil and was better able to face my issues.

Fanny suggested that a sharing circle can be a healing circle. However, she also recognized that there are slight variations in the types of circles, but "it's really hard to pinpoint." Bernie was more strong in voicing that there is a difference in sharing and healing circles. She stated:

> Well, I've participated in healing circles. They're different. They are usually conducted by an Elder and they're different in that the Elder can actually speak to what you're talking about, whereas if you're running a sharing circle the facilitator doesn't give you direction about how you're, what you're talking about, whereas an Elder can actually talk to you in a healing circle, give you some direction on things that you might be able to do to either get rid of some of the hurt, the anger, the pain, whatever, is able to help you with that more.

When I participated in sharing circles, there were times when other participants referred to the circle as a healing circle. Neither the conductors nor any other participants made a correction that the circles were not healing circles. It was my impression that if a participant wanted to call a particular circle a healing circle, it was up to them. What seems most significant was whether it was the intent of the circle participants or conductor to include a healing aspect. In one particular circle in which I participated the conductors were two Elders. I recall a difference in this circle in that the participants seemed to be asking more questions during their turn to speak. They seemed focused on intense issues and were looking for guidance from others, particularly the Elders. I also recall that the Elders spoke more about healing generally, and their own healing experiences specifically. In other circles where the intent was on healing, there were individuals trained to use the circle for healing, and there were traditional medicines such as sweetgrass included in the process.

Learning in Circles
Sharing circles also involve a learning process. Katz and St. Denis (1991) suggest that circles have been used by Cree communities to develop greater community understanding. The community gathers in a circle, or as if in a

circle, and places a topic metaphorically in the middle of the circle. From this place, the topic is seen from all vantage points of the circle surrounding it. Each person present has an opportunity to present their view on the topic. The views are blended into a shared experience until there is consensus on their shared insight. This process draws on the trans-personal knowledge of the community, as well as respecting each person's contributions. Katz and St. Denis also suggest that there is an exponentially greater understanding of the topic by all members. More specifically, if something, whether real or abstract, is placed in the centre of the circle, everyone's unique perspective adds to the understanding of the object or idea. As the number of people in the circle reflecting upon the object increases, so does the complexity and depth of the understanding of the object.

As evident from this outline of the development of a community understanding and according to Aboriginal worldviews, everyone is mutually a teacher *and* a learner, even while in a sharing circle (Hart 1996; Katz and St. Denis 1991). In order to teach and learn from others in the circle, participants, which includes the members and the conductor, are required to have humility, strength and courage:

> This is my understanding of strength, the strength to acknowledge that while all the relationships that surround us do not *need* us, we have a responsibility to contribute to them positively as long as we remain within them.... Sometimes it takes sitting in a circle with people who have, despite horrible beginnings in their lives, found the courage to move farther up that healing mountain than you ever imagined anyone could go. Whatever it takes, this combination of humility, strength and courage seems to be the only way to open you up enough to start learning who and what you might become. (Ross 1996: 191, emphasis in the original)

In each of the sharing circles in which I participated, there was at least one person who commented on their learning that had taken place in the circle. Indeed, in several, if not all, of the circles I learned something. For example, in one particular circle, participants gathered to speak on a common issue, namely Aboriginal worldviews. Throughout the sharing process each person gave a perspective that I had only minimally, if ever, considered before. This circle carried on for two days, during which time I had several opportunities to share. After I spoke it seemed that some people would pick up on what I had said and add to it. It was as if the concept of Aboriginal worldviews was building as each person, including myself, commented on it. In this manner, I felt as if I was in process of continuous learning about Aboriginal worldviews.

In regards to the learning that occurs in circles, Fanny was the only conductor to discuss a connection between sharing, learning and teaching circles. Fanny suggested that "sharing circles are learning circles too. So, you learn things from there." However, she also mentioned that teaching circles are still somewhat different than sharing circles in that a particular concept is presented in order to learn about it. She also identified that the conductor would have the intent to teach about a particular concept. In this regard, the sharing circle that I participated in, where the concept of Aboriginal worldviews was the main topic being discussed, could be considered a teaching circle.

Glen saw the process as one of continuous learning: "For me, the whole experience of the sharing circle is continuous learning." Marg also emphasized the learning process of sharing circles:

> Well, to me sharing circles are a process of learning. Passing on information is very vital to a group of people because ... a long time ago when our ancestors did not have communication airways, they communicated in this manner. It could be various types of people, like in one key location, or they may be outside tribes surrounding that little area. So in order for everybody to benefit by what's happening ... [they would follow] the purpose of having a sharing circle [which] was to have these people pulled in together and talk about new information.

Glen also acknowledged that all people benefit from the sharing of information:

> It works both ways. We share a lot of different information. And so, it's a learning process. Everything is continuously learning, you know. And I can see the value of whether it's a talking circle, sharing circle, whatever term that you want to call it, you know, it still has great value.

He also added that whether or not someone does something with the information is up to each individual:

> So, you know, for me the same thing would basically happen in the sharing circle. I would say if the sharing circle is provided with

information that would be helpful in their learning, whether it's through a small presentation beforehand or someone just talking about it in the circle, then that will create an awareness for the group, for the circle. And once they have that, then the choice is theirs as to what they want to do with it.

In addition to learning from one another, Bernie noted that when people who have faced similar experiences share their life stories with one another, they become connected and their experiences are validated. She suggested that this connection and validation is a step in their learning and in their growth process. Indeed, Morrissette et al. (1993) notes that shared experiences, particularly the painful ones, can lead the participants to collective action to change the common situations that the people face.

Bernie and Fanny emphasized that circle participants need to practise respect in order to learn. In addition, Marg stressed the need to watch and listen in order to learn. She stated "you learn through seeing, being able to visualize what's happening through hearing." Similarly, individuals need to open their mind's eye as well as their heart (Glen).

Once people are open to learning and are willing to take information that may benefit them, then a variety of skills can be learned through sharing circles. Glen noted that amongst the first things learned are basic listening and attending:

> So this is what ties in with what I'm seeing in sharing circles, you know. You're learning to respect the person who's talking. You're learning to develop your listening skills. Truly listen to the individuals. Whether there's feedback required in the process, that's up to the group. It's still, it all ties in with that. So for me the whole experience of the sharing circle is continuous learning and in being sensitive.

He added:

> And basically it was just listening, that's it. Just listening. Paraphrasing, summarizing, but not giving any information unless it was asked for. So, you know I'm learning all these things, I thought, it all comes down to the basic process we have here with sharing circles. This is that learning vehicle, this is a learning tool right here.

Marg noted that two of the basic communication skills she learned through sharing circles were patience and the ability to be quiet.

Bernie identified an experience where the participants once again learned to think for themselves. She explained that the participants began "to explore who they are, what they think.... And so for them it was a real learning experience about who they are and to begin to think about what their thoughts were." Similarly, Marg noted that sharing circles supported her to learn how to analyze. They also supported young men and women to learn about their responsibilities and preparation for entering adulthood. Glen identified a variety of things people learn from sharing circles, including how to identify, connect with and express their feelings with honesty and responsibility.

It was noted by Bernie that the opportunity to learn these things is not limited to only the participants. In her experience as a conductor of sharing circles she has learned as well. She stated, "It's not like I'm the teacher and I know everything. I'm there to learn as much as I'm, I'm sharing. As much as I can get from the stories that I hear too that I learn a lot."

A Circular Worldview

One of the most evident, at times striking, features of the sharing circles which I participated in was the circular worldview based upon spirituality. While a sharing circle can reach the fourth level, identified by Antone and Hill (1990) as being the spiritual circle where people use their intuition and practices to begin to reclaim their spiritual guides, in one way or another, all sharing circles incorporate some spiritual expression. As Alice Modig (cited in Scott 1991) suggests, the spiritual realm is unavoidable because so many symbols are present in the circle. The degree to which traditional Aboriginal spirituality is included can vary since circles may or may not include sacred items or spiritual ceremonies (Clarkson et al. 1992; Hart 1996; Scott 1991). Overall, these points coincide with the understanding held by the conductors, Glen in particular, that the fundamental philosophy behind sharing circles was a spiritual one based upon circular worldviews.

To begin, sharing circles are, or can be, very sacred. Fanny, Marg and Bernie each identified that the inclusion of prayer and symbols, such as feathers, stones, talking sticks and blessed ribbons, make circles sacred. Bernie suggested, "I think what smudging rituals do is help people focus, really focus on what they're doing, on their own growth. I find it's more special for them to participate in the smudging ceremony as well. It becomes more sacred." She added that sharing circles are also made sacred through the confidentiality that is maintained. Fanny stated, "So for me sharing circles are very spiritual. So to me it's a spiritual ceremony and I feel that if smudging is not a part of that, somehow it's cold, and there's a little bit of an emptiness or a bleakness. You know, something is stark." She also added that placing cedar behind the people in the circle also adds to making the circle a very special place.

Glen and Bernie noted that not all people see sharing circles as sacred. Bernie noted that some people, "because of their Christian beliefs," associate sharing circles and smudging with traditional Aboriginal spirituality and as such, view them as wrong, evil or pagan. Glen recalled one particular community, which was strongly aligned to a particular church, that was "not so enthusiastic" about traditional activities. However, Bernie also noticed that some individuals who hold such views have also been able to consider other perspectives:

> Some of these women have never experienced anything with tradition or they have negative images of what traditional spirituality means. Within that circle they get fed, you know. They begin to understand that [traditional Aboriginal] spirituality is okay. It's not pagan. It's not evil. It's not all of those things.

In one of the sharing circles which I attended, several people remained very cautious about participating. They emphasized regularly that they were strong Christians. In order to accommodate them, this particular sharing circle did not include any smudging. I also noted that the few people who addressed the topic of traditional spirituality in this circle were very cautious when they spoke. In other circles I noticed people's passion towards the sharing circle as a sacred ceremony. In these circles, there was smudging, placing of sacred bundles in the centre, and open sharing about beliefs. In some of these circles, there were also some people who identified themselves as strong Christians. They still participated fully and gave thanks for being able to participate. There was a great sense of comfort and ease in these circles. It also appeared to me that when smudging, sacred objects and prayer were included, there was a sense of sacredness to the circles. People seemed to be more respectful, listened more intently, were less disruptive and more frequently spoke about the Creator and spirituality. They had reverence for the process.

Several of the conductors noted that beyond the physical presence of the participants, there is acknowledgement of spiritual others. For example, Mary noted:

> You're not the only one that comes [to the circle], you bring your family, you bring your people that have even gone on. So it's not only what you see. So I get that sense of, how do you say, some spiritual side. Spirit side. That's what I get from there too.

Another example was given by Glen:

> The spirit world, our spiritual guides, our spiritual helpers, angels if you will, if you want to use Christian terms, are what guides us and directs us in this life here when we're lost. Now they will always be there. Like the Elders, the traditional healers that I've worked with and learned from for four to five years say that when we come into the physical world, every single human being has a grandfather and that grandfather will watch over them and guide them.

It was also noted that these spiritual others can be requested to support: "You ask the grandfathers to come in and heal the person" (Glen). On the same point Fanny explained in more detail: "So what do you do with all the pain and the hurt that's being shared. It needs to be taken care of. I always, for me, think that it needs to be somehow offered or allowed or acknowledged that Mother Earth or grandfathers will take care of all of that and we don't have to take it back."

I noticed that during several of the circles in which I participated people stated that they have prayed and asked for support from the Creator. At other times people said that "the grandfathers have watched over and guided them." In one particular circle, the conductor suggested at the beginning of the circle that if someone felt any pain or hurt during the ceremony that they should pray and ask the Creator to help them through that time. This same conductor also told the participants that when the opening prayer was being said, they could say their own prayers to the Creator and grandfathers and ask them to support everyone in the circle.

While people may reach out to the spiritual others, or grandfathers, for support, they are viewed as still holding responsibilities. For example, Glen shared part of a conversation he had with an Elder: "Basically that was his whole point. That you are responsible for your own path. No one else is. The guidance and direction will come from the grandfathers or grandmother, Creator, in those ways that you, that you've been taught."

When asking for help, Glen noted that people are trying to get support to overcome any barriers to healing that they might have. These barriers are self-created. He stated as an example, "People will create their own barriers by saying, 'well, Joe Bloe over there looks like someone I don't like so I'm not going to open up here.' That to me is a mental model that creates hindrance. So [I need] to release this energy or this emotion that's stopping me from healing." Mary acknowledged that this energy exists and that it may be negative. Fanny noted this energy on a group level and that the grandfathers can be called upon to help take care of it:

> Sometimes maybe there is resentment or anger or fear or something that I want to let go. I think a sharing circle is a good place to let it go. And I think that whoever is leading or facilitating should somehow offer it to grandfathers. Because I've been to circles and it sits there. And somehow the circles kind of just fall apart. I think we come together with a great purpose in a circle and so the circle must also, I think, at least when these circles decide to separate, then it [the ending] needs to be done in a very strong way. Whatever business is there in the air ... the energy needs to be taken care of. I think that helps.

It was suggested by Glen that when this energy is not dealt with people run the risk of becoming ill:

> Emotions are energy and if you don't learn how to express energy, then that energy doesn't go anywhere ... because that energy doesn't go anywhere and it stays in the body, then that leads into the energy creating kidney infections, liver infections, heart infections and some muscles, you know, the bones. And everything gets infected because that energy isn't going anywhere. That negative energy. That anger. The hurt. The pain isn't moving. It isn't discharging from the body.

He further suggested that if the energy is not released, then a person's "doorways" to centredness, balance and harmony are blocked.

The concept of releasing certain energies was also addressed in some of the sharing circles where I was a participant. In the sharing circle where I felt extremely overwhelmed with the anger fear and sadness that seemed to be present in the circle, I was encouraged to release this energy and to feel free to cry. In another circle, I recall that a participant spoke about the connection between getting sick frequently and the inability to release grief.

In addition to releasing this energy by reaching out to the Creator and grandfathers, it was also important to connect with the four aspects within ourselves, namely the spiritual, emotional, physical and mental. Glen suggested that in the present time people have focused upon the physical and mental realms and avoided connecting with the spiritual and emotional realms. He repeatedly emphasized that "we've got to move towards that in all aspects. That's what we've got to get in touch with is learning how to feel. Learning how to connect with our spirit." He also noted that people have to work on all parts of themselves at the same time and through this work we move to becoming more balanced and in harmony:

> There's this balance and harmony and, you know, to bring out all those parts of myself in terms of the four aspects. You know you have the emotional, the physical, the mental and the spiritual. Um. It's about coming to balance with all aspects of self.... And everything. And for me to begin my journey I need to explore each of those doorways.

This concept of becoming balanced and in harmony was repeatedly addressed in most of the sharing circles that I attended. For example, balance and harmony were key topics in the sharing circle which addressed Aboriginal worldviews.

In attempting to release energy and establish connections, balance and harmony, ceremonies—including sharing circles—play a significant part. For example, Mary and Fanny indirectly noted that there were ceremonies that help people to release energy. They identified such ceremonies as healing ceremonies (Fanny) and grieving ceremonies (Mary). Glen identified that ceremonies help him to release energy, connect with others and become centered:

> You know when you're in that sweat lodge or when you're in that sun dance, you're connected as a circle, both at a conscious level and an unconscious level. We're all connected and for me it all ties right back into the sharing circle. I'm moving through each of these experiences. All four aspects of self, the journey to the true self, the centre, the centre of the universe, is me, the centre of the universe is you, those people sitting over there. That's where the journey is. So, if I need to get in touch with those parts of myself, then I need a place or a vehicle that will allow me to do that. And sharing circles will allow that.

Glen also gave an encompassing clarification that "all our ceremonies are about right brain phenomenon. You know, accessing the spiritual, the emotional, the dreams, the vision, the holistic thinking." In other words, all ceremonies act to help people release energy, make connections with each other and within, and bring about balance and harmony. They act to bring each person "to the centre which is the Creator or the Great Spirit that is in the centre of me and you and everybody else and everything."

At times, ceremonies are used one after the other as a way to help people become centred. Mary, Fanny and Glen each noted that pipe ceremonies may immediately precede a sharing circle or that sweat lodge ceremonies may include a sharing circle. There was a pipe ceremony in three of the sharing circles that I participated in. While none of the sharing circles that I participated in occurred in association with a sweat lodge ceremony, I have participated in sweat lodge ceremonies that have included sharing circles.

Ceremonies help establish connectedness and balance and help harmonize a person's physical, emotional, spiritual and mental aspects, not only within but also beyond the individual. These processes can extend to groups of people; by coming together, people can experience being one entity. Sharing circles support this level of connection, balancing, harmony and holism. For example, Marg suggested that sharing circles bring harmony to the group. Mary identified that people in circles experience "feelings of, um, belonging somewhere … a chance to become one." Glen made a similar comment:

> So it works, I know, for people who are becoming in tune with this energy. So again it goes back to that circle. People with a connection as one. Because isn't that one of the basic teachings of our whole philosophy is that we're all one. Right. We're all one. One spirit in a sense. We're all one, you know, the unconscious, the subconscious are all connected as one.

In one particular circle I felt a strong sense of connection and commitment. I also felt that I belonged to this group of people and that they would truly do whatever they could to support me. When people spoke it seemed like I clearly understood their experiences and felt their feelings. When the circle came to a close it was as if something was ending, almost dying. People felt so strongly towards one another that when some of them hugged, they cried and held on to one another for awhile. Something that stood out to me during this time of departure was when someone said something to the effect of, "Take good care of my heart because you are carrying part of it with you." This circle was different than most of the others in that the level of connection and empathy was far deeper and more intense.

It appears that what helped develop this level of connection and empathy, as well as guiding the circles overall, was a worldview that emphasizes cycles and circles. Marg and the people who taught her about such things as sharing circles believe that "everything goes in a circle." Fanny also noted the importance of circles in the people's view: "Why is that so important? I guess it's life. So you have birth and you have your life cycle and then you move into another, you know, onto the other side or to another plane, you die, you leave this earth and go to the spiritual world. All that's a cycle. So that's how we live I guess is in cycles." Glen also shared why he thought circles are important:

> So for me, not going into detail with it is one of the things that I see why the circle is so important. The circle itself, whether it's with the Aboriginal people, or like any other culture in the world that have it in their culture in one way or another. You know, whether the mandala or some other form, the symbol itself is as prominent throughout many cultures. So that's how I see that. That it creates this unison, this unity, at a conscious level and an unconscious level. That's the purpose of that. All are one, all are connected. All our prayers are focused.

Sharing circles contain a variety of symbols reflective of Aboriginal spiritual worldviews. The circle itself was noted by Fanny, Glen and Bernie as a symbol of cooperation, equality and life. Fanny and Glen identified that the earth is seen as our mother. Spirits are our grandfathers and/or our relatives. Doorways exist where people can enter and move from the physical to the spiritual realm. Bernie spoke of how the rock that is passed around sharing circles symbolizes the earth. She also spoke of water as "symbolic of life." Glen noted that when circle participants hold an eagle feather and speak, they are "actually verbalizing themselves as a form of a prayer." He later added:

> So, for me, that's how I see it. The individual holding that feather is actually in a form of prayer with the Creator, with other human beings, with all things, with mother earth, and with the grandfathers who are found in the four cardinal directions, everything,

you know. And I'm owning what I'm saying. I'm holding that feather and that feather represents honesty and integrity as well. So you see, it all ties in with that. The rock is another thing too. It can be used for destruction, or it can be used to build.

In ten of the twelve sharing circles I attended there was some overt form of symbolism. For example, in four of them water was placed in the middle of the circle. In one of these circles it was explained that water was representative of life. In another sharing circle there was a lit candle placed in the middle, which was said to represent a campfire as well as life. Fanny suggested that these symbols make sharing circles more sacred, provide comfort and offer reassurance. She shared a significant story that reflected the incorporation of symbols in the sharing circles she conducts:

And so what, I remember one time there was a fairly large group.... And so you work things out so that everybody has a chance to speak. So time was very important. Sometimes people are very reluctant [to speak]. Not every group will behave the same way to this process. This was a teaching circle.... I had put a blanket out in the centre of the circle and offered to those who shared that what we would share, our thoughts and our feelings, will go towards the centre of the circle [on to the blanket]. We all agreed to be together. Time was going on and in this particular session, people were talking really talking and they seemed to be feeling comfortable. But we needed to take a break. And so then there was a chance to take a break, probably after a round. That's the other thing, you can always come and go I think at a sharing circle. But sometimes it's very hard to leave a circle when people are talking and so you gave a break.... People were glad. They wanted to take a break without missing anything. [At the break] a woman was talking to me and she was backing up and her feet were starting to touch the blanket [in the centre of the circle]. There were other people who didn't leave the room and saw her backing up towards the blanket. They said, "Watch it, watch it, watch it, you're stepping on our feelings." [chuckle] So she jumped and she turned around and said, "Oh, I'm sorry, I'm sorry." She bent over the blanket and smoothed it. And they said, "Yes, look at that, you're just pushing our feelings around." So she bent down and she started a scooping motion with her hands to symbolize plac-ing the feelings back onto the blanket. She says, "here," she says,

"I didn't want to, didn't mean to knock these off." You know, she was sort of making a motion that the feelings should be going back onto the blanket, you know, so it was very interesting for me to see. There is this respect for feelings. The feelings are something that can be seen and that are almost tangible. And so when they were talking, some of them had seen it. Their thoughts and stories were actually put out for everybody to see and that they should be taken care of, so you don't step on them and knock them off the blanket. So I liked that story. So then at the end I made sure that I went over and asked people to take what they wanted back, take care of whatever it was they shared because there might be another time that they choose to take these stories out again. Then those things that they didn't want to take, I said, "Well, I'll ask, I can't remember who, to take care of them." You know. And so then you make motions with your hands and they will take. And so people are glad. 'Cause sometimes they don't want to take a resentment with them, you know, just leave it there, you know, so I think it's important that it be taken. Other times I've said I'll take them in this blanket and put them off some place safe. I've done that too. And so people think that's good. Well taken care, even the resentments and their anger but they are taken care of and it was nice to let go. So, anyway, so you can't shake the blanket, you know. So I always make sure I fold up this blanket and unfold it in a very deliberate way. I use candles too, and water.

SHARING CIRCLES AND AN ABORIGINAL APPROACH

It is clear that sharing circles hold the same the foundational concepts and values of an Aboriginal approach. Indeed, the essence of sharing circles is the process of seeking *mino-pimatisiwin* as they rest on the concepts, values and worldviews held in the Aboriginal approach to helping. An Aboriginal approach is made up of several foundational concepts that stem from the medicine wheel. These include wholeness, balance, relationships between all parts, harmony, growth, healing and the primary goal of *mino-pimatisiwin*. Each of these concepts was discussed by the conductors I spoke with and/or observed in my participation in sharing circles. The importance of wholeness was demonstrated when an Elder outlined that it was important to close the gaps in the sharing circles so that people would be brought closer together and unified as one. Glen identified that balance is addressed in circles when individuals work on connecting themselves emotionally, mentally, physically and spiritually. He also discussed three other concepts when he identified that ceremonies, including sharing circles, help establish balance, harmony and centredness. Healing was a very significant topic discussed by the conductors. For example, they focused much of our discussions on the belief that healing comes about through emotional expression, discharging turmoil and through cleansing and purifying oneself.

The Aboriginal approach's key supporting values of respect, sharing and spirituality were identified as being a part of sharing circles. Mary identified that respecting everyone was a basic rule of sharing circles, while Fanny said that each person deserves to be respected. The value of sharing is one of the primary functions of sharing circles. For example, Marg explained that sharing circles are learning processes where people "share a lot of different information." Indeed, sharing is such an important factor that all circles are noted for their sharing aspects. The value of spirituality was acknowledged by Mary when she explained that she senses a spiritual side to sharing circles. Spirituality also was highlighted by all of the conductors who reflected upon the use of spiritual ceremonies, such as prayers and smudging.

The perception of people as outlined in an Aboriginal approach is demonstrated in sharing circles. In one sharing circle that I participated in, the conductor acknowledged both good and bad aspects of life and encouraged people to focus on the positive. Bernie noted how the state of being was emphasized in sharing circles when she stated that people "really focus on what they are doing." The state of being-in-becoming was indirectly acknowledged when Glen identified that sharing circles have value in that they support people in their continuous learning. Glen also supported the point that people have a flexible sense of time as demonstrated by their willingness to look at the past, present and future and how they influence each other. For example, he talked about how he was "processing his past relationship with his step father" in a sharing circle. He also talked about how people in sharing circles must deal with emotions they are experiencing or else they run the risk of being sick in the future. In other words, people are actively striving to accept and understand their present situation while working to develop themselves through continuous learning and healing. While it was not overtly noted that people are purposeful, this was indirectly identified in people's attempts to become more balanced and in harmony through such processes as healing and learning. As Bernie stated, relationships are very significant in that people were seen as being one entity when they come together in a sharing circle. They can feel a sense of inclusion and belonging.

In their discussions, the conductors I spoke with demonstrated that sharing circles incorporated a view of peoples functioning that matches that of an Aboriginal approach. For example, Bernie identified the importance of the history of sharing circles. Cycles were noted by Marg to be symbolically present in sharing circles since they followed cyclical patterns such as the movement of the sun. Glen noted that people connect in circles consciously and unconsciously. He also noted that people can go through changes in sharing circles by letting go of "the garbage" that is holding them back. Sharing circles demonstrate that the motivation for changes lies within individuals, since participation, including whether someone speaks, is voluntary. Also, people are not to interfere with one another. As Glen stated, "the choice is theirs," as to what people do with the information they gain in circles.

Sharing circles follow a helping process that is reflected in an Aboriginal approach. There is emphasis on the relationships between people in the circle. For example, Marg explained that interfering when someone speaks is unacceptable. Instead, all people are to respect one another. Further, people are to validate each other's feelings, thoughts, and experiences by paying attention and not pressuring others to finish. Sharing circles also demonstrate the interdependent relationship people hold. People are involved in a shared experience of learning and growing. Indeed, Marg identified that the purpose of having some sharing circles was to have people pull together and talk about new information in order for everybody to benefit from the information.

Sharing circles incorporate the same techniques identified in an Aboriginal approach. Humour is incorporated since, as Glen highlights, laughter brings people together. Ceremonies are also aligned with sharing circles—for example, the performances of a smudge ceremony immediately before the circle. Storytelling is incorporated in sharing circles, as described in Fanny's example of when she was a child listening to people tell stories as they sat in a circle. People also act as role models for one another in sharing circles. Bernie noted that when people have faced and overcome certain experiences they validate others in their journey through similar experiences. Elders are often conductors of sharing circles. Whether conducted by Elders or others, circles are usually led by individuals, such as Marg, Mary, Glen, Fanny and Bernie, who have gone through training and preparation. Conductors have learned such skills as the ability to centre themselves. They are to be kind, gentle, moral, ethical, confident, strong, flexible, good listeners, patient, accommodating and respectful. Indirectly it was noted that the conductors do not direct other people; instead they support people to determine their own goals.

CHAPTER FIVE

AN ABORIGINAL APPROACH IN PRACTICE

An Aboriginal approach to helping is orientated to general applications. It can guide helpers to work with individuals, families and groups. It supports helpers and individuals in addressing a variety of issues, such as family violence and self-development. This approach can also be used in conjunction with other applications and theories that have similar foundations. This chapter gives an overview of how an Aboriginal approach is generally applied in a variety of situations. In this overview the foundational concepts of holism, balance, connection between all parts, harmony, growth, healing and *mino-pimatisiwin,* as well as the values of sharing, respect and spirituality, are addressed. It is important to recognize that each of these applications has a common beginning for helpers, namely themselves.

THE HELPER IN PRACTICE

Helpers following an Aboriginal approach recognize that they are role models of positive growth and well-being. Thus, helpers begin the helping process by addressing themselves. They prepare themselves to help others by establishing and maintaining an awareness of their own emotional, mental, spiritual and physical well-being. They work at balancing and connecting these aspects within themselves as they, themselves, strive towards *mino-pimatisiwin.* For example, while learning about how to help others and how to follow an Aboriginal approach, they would also be physically active, finding and/or reaffirming their own sense of spirituality and expressing a range of emotions appropriately. They also see their own wellness in relation to the wellness of their own families, communities and nations. They recognize that if they are unhealthy, they will find it difficult to support their own family. If they are in denial of their own neglectful behaviours towards their families, they will face difficulties in addressing the neglectful behaviours of the people they are helping. The importance of maintaining harmony within themselves and with their families, communities and nations is also recognized. They try to ensure that the many hours learning required to become a helper does not stop them from maintaining a healthy degree of physical activity or contributing to their family's well-being. Their contribution to the wellness of their community or to the development of their nation is done in a way which maintains their support of their own families' well-being.

Helpers raise and maintain an awareness of their personal histories. They understand the histories of their own family, community and nation and how they are influenced by these histories. The helpers' values, which include respect and sharing, are clear to them. They model such values by sharing their knowledge, experiences and abilities in a way which respects the abilities and gifts of others. For example, a helper may share their personal story of how they coped with a violent family member in order to inform another person of a way to address their similar experience. Such a story is clearly given as an option and is brought into the person's context. In this way, the helper tries to respect the person's ability to determine her or his own life path.

Their sense of spirituality is well established and used as a guide in their life journey towards *mino-pimatisiwin*. They may be involved in their own cultural ways of spirituality or committed to an organized religion's manner of worship that respects Aboriginal cultures. While acknowledging both the bad and good aspects within and around themselves, these helpers focus on the positive aspects of life. They strive to learn from the hardships they have faced and caused, and use what they have learned for healing and growth. They recognize difficult situations, problems and pain created by the structures in our society and by people in distress. They also see the beauty of discovery, healing and growth within themselves and in the universe around them and as such pull out the opportunities for healing and growth that these difficulties, problems and pains provide. They acknowledge the role that rituals and ceremonies have in this process and they utilize them for help and support. They also seek out support and guidance from Elders and other people who have travelled further along their own life journeys. These individuals may be sought to provide cultural teachings to address issues such as those stemming from cultural degradation. They may also be asked to provide insight to help the individuals strive towards *mino-pimatisiwin*.

Upon initiating a focus on themselves and working to maintain a degree of balance, connection and harmony for healing and growth, helpers are in a better position to follow an Aboriginal approach when helping others. Indeed, such self-reflection and action become a component of the helping process and can be used within it. As such, they are prepared and willing to share their own experiences of growth with people, including those seeking help. They see their role of helper as part of their journey—one in which they learn about themselves as people and as participants in a relationship. They remain patient and take the time to develop a personable, if not personal, relationship with the people. They see themselves as persons with abilities, not experts, in the helping process. Helpers acknowledge that their own journeys will be supported by what the people share with them, thus adding to the respect that they hold of the people. They also acknowledge that in the sharing of their own lives, including what they learned to prepare as helpers, they can support others in their healing and growth.

HELPING INDIVIDUALS

Helpers recognize that they need to develop an understanding of each individual they are working with, including that person's personal, family, community and national history and how that history affects the present. To develop this understanding, helpers closely listen to the life story of each individual. They also develop an awareness of each individual's emotional, physical, mental and spiritual wellness as seen by the individual. They seek to hear about and support the individual in all relationships they hold.

Once the relationship between the helper and the person seeking help is accepted and established, the helper supports the individual in self-reflection processes that are based upon holisitic wellness. They encourage the person seeking help to reflect upon matters such as whether they are able to express a full range of emotions in ways that are appropriate to their culture, whether they take physical care of themselves, meet cognitive challenges and actively learn, and whether they feel and express their sense of spirituality. For example, an individual who tries to avoid feelings of sadness is encouraged to consider the reason for suppressing them and the role such feelings play for individuals, for their families and for society. As another example, an individual whose diet consists of junk food is encouraged to reflect upon the body's need for proper nutrition and what happens to a person holistically if they do receive adequate nutrients.

Helpers also guide people to consider how they can strengthen their relationships with their families, communities and nations, and contribute to the wellness of the people who are directly and indirectly involved in their lives. For example, an individual who holds tightly onto all of the family responsibilities, such as the family finances, may be encouraged to think about what this models for the development of responsibility in their children. Helpers also encourage people to consider their relationships with the natural environment and the land and how these relationships can support the growth of all considered. Reflecting upon such matters as taking leisurely walks in parks may help individuals to see that they are influenced by the environment around them and encourage them to take a more active stance in the well-being of the environment. They may also be better able to see the inter-connection between all life and the responsibility to others that we all hold.

This self-reflection, or self-assessment process is also used to help people to establish their own goals for the helping process, as well as to establish centredness. The dreams and visions of the people seeking help is incorporated into the process of determining goals. Helpers may be asked to interpret dreams, but unless they have special training they limit their support to helping people determine their own meaning or find someone who does interpret dreams. Helpers encourage a positive focus for both the self-assessment and the establishment of goals. Individuals who are caught on negative self-images are reminded of their gifts, abilities and achievements. Throughout the goal development period, the helper acknowledges the future but maintains a focus in the present by recognizing the realities that people are experiencing. To help individuals meet their goals, helpers incorporate techniques such as humour and role modelling through the direct and indirect sharing of life experiences. When sharing stories and past life experiences, indeed throughout the helping relationship, helpers speak from their hearts. The use of helping theories are screened through the helpers' personal experiences, thus making the relationship more personal and limiting textbook or policy-driven responses.

Elders are sought by helpers for their supervision, support, direction and/or as direct resources for the people seeking help. If desired by people seeking help and the helper, ceremonies are used within some or all sessions. For example, a smudging ceremony in which cleansing plant medicines are burnt and the smoke is used to wash the participants may be conducted. The people seeking help and, if possible, the helper may participate in traditional ceremonies, such as sweats or sharing circles conducted by Aboriginal healers or Elders. Helpers also support participation in other ceremonies and rituals that are respectful, helpful and deemed important by people, regardless of whether they are from another culture or created by the individuals themselves.

As people continue to journey, there comes a time when the helping process comes to an end. This ending will include a symbolic ritual, which may be simple or elaborate, to signal a change in the relationship. In this ending process, helpers support individuals to see that the cycle of their relationship has come full circle and recognize that it will take on a new direction and meaning in the future. This meaning may involve further contact or it may mean only reflections on the relationship. Thus, helpers accept that people may turn to them in the future, may cross their path in other ways or may never see them again. In other words, even after the helping processes are finished, helpers continue to rely on an Aboriginal approach to guide their actions.

A Case Example with an Individual Focus[1]

James Maskwa was a young man in his early twenties. He had come to speak with me about his loneliness and depression. He was told that he was originally from a First Nation that was accessible by road but several hours away from where he now lived, a major city in the province. He was the youngest of a fairly large family originally consisting of his mother, father, three brothers and two sisters. He and his siblings were taken from his family when he was four years old. He was told the reason for their removal was that his mother had died and his father subsequently began binge drinking. He was placed alone with a non-Aboriginal foster family in the city. Apparently, no family was able to accommodate him and his siblings together. He was later adopted by his foster family.

While his childhood was comfortable in that his adoptive parents and two adoptive siblings accepted him as "one of their own" and attempted to meet his basic needs, his teenage years were marked by many turbulent times. He became withdrawn and overweight. His grades changed from just above average to below average and failing. He avoided school functions and extra-curricular activities. Later, he began spending summer nights away from home, usually alone in parks. On one of these occasions he tried drinking "some hard stuff" but became violently ill. This event was enough to stop him from drinking in the future. On another occasion, James cut the word "loser" into his arm with a broken bottle. At this point his parents took him to see a psychologist. After a several months of counselling, James had stopped running from home and was attending school regularly. While he managed to interact with his adoptive family and present a front of contentment, his personal sense of aloneness and depression continued.

He managed to finish high school by the age of twenty. Upon graduating he worked in several jobs, ranging from pizza delivery driver, dishwasher and prep-cook to a labourer in a lawn maintenance company. None of these jobs lasted more than six months. Just prior to coming to see me, he was considering taking a course at a local college. He had completed filling out the application form and was set to receive financial support from his adoptive parents. However, when the due date for the application arrived, he spent the entire day and evening in the park. Upon learning of the missed application, his older adoptive sister called him "lazy" and yelled at his adoptive parents to throw him out of the house. After this incident, James began withdrawing once again. Recalling a pamphlet describing the counselling agency in which I worked, his adoptive father encouraged James to call to arrange an appointment. James agreed but with little enthusiasm.

Prior to working with James, I had already gone through a general self-reflection process. This process continued and became more specific as I spent more time with James and as my understanding of James's life developed. I considered my own experiences with the child welfare system, the periods when I was away from my mother and my efforts to overcome my own experiences of sadness or depression. The self-reflection first and foremost served to develop a repertoire of stories which I tapped into and utilized for James's benefit. At the same time, I recognized that my time with James would also have the effect of supporting my development as a helper and an individual. As such, I maintained my respect for and honour of James for what he was sharing with me.

Among the first requirements in our process was the establishment of a personal working relationship with James. This required me to remain true to my own sense of self while maintaining my professional character. Explicitly tied to this process was the development of my knowledge of James's situation and life story as explained by James. I explored with James each aspect of his well-being, including his physical, emotional, spiritual and mental states. To give this understanding some context, I encouraged James to developed as deeply as possible his understanding of his personal story and the history of his adoptive and biological families. He was encouraged to reflect upon his formative years, to recall family stories and to ask his family questions about their experiences together. I was also prepared to support James in seeking out information from the child welfare system about his biological family and his community of origin; this came later in the form of accessing information for him on how to approach the system.

Recalling the Aboriginal approach's guiding concept of relationships between all aspects of life, I encouraged James to think about the inter-relationships between the emotional, physical, mental and spiritual, as well as individual, familial, communal and national parts of his life. We discussed how he was balancing each of these aspects in relation to each of the others. For instance, we spent time exploring how his physical wellness, specifically him being overweight, influenced his emotional well-being and vice versa. We also discussed whether his being adopted by a non-Aboriginal family and moving to a new community influenced him emotionally.

From this self-assessment process, James came to see how he was carrying feelings of rejection and, despite all the efforts of his adoptive family, how he never overcame these feelings. He recognized that his physical appearance and well-being were tied to these feelings of rejection, in that he hated to see himself as an Aboriginal person. He recalled that he would eat to comfort himself at these times, especially when he reached his teenage years. In this way, he did not have to work at his relationship with his adoptive family, particularly since he knew he could never be like them physically. He recalled how he wanted to hide from everyone and that the places which were easiest to escape to were his room and, later, the park. During the helping process, he spoke of how he did not fit in his school community, especially when taunted about his identity. He came to recognize that while he was able to understand what was taught to him, his thoughts were preoccupied with these feelings of not fitting in. This was the root of his academic concerns. He also recognized that his slow academic progress only fed his low self-esteem and left him feeling incompetent, despite his graduation from high school. By looking at each aspect of his life and seeing the relationships between them, James developed a more holistic understanding of himself. Yet at that time in the helping process, James acknowledged that he still felt unhappy and uncertain about himself and his future.

To help James further, I got his consent to consult an Elder about his experiences. At the Elder's suggestion and with James's agreement, I escorted James to meet with the Elder. I prepared James by talking to him about the role an Elder may fulfil in the helping process, how to approach the Elder in an appropriate manner, and some possible ways in which the Elder might respond. After listening to James, the Elder spent much time with James and me. The Elder was able to provide James with a little information about his community of origin, confirmed James's understanding that he was Cree and gave some directions to both of us on our next steps in the helping process.

We spent the following period supporting James to discover his Cree roots. James did go the child welfare system to access information on himself and his family. Our time together changed focus to helping James established a sense of himself as a Cree man raised within a non-Aboriginal family. We began this change with a small ceremony as suggested by the Elder. This involved putting on a feast which his adoptive family, the Elder and I attended. During this feast James presented his intention of accepting and developing himself within the context of his adoptive family and his Cree heritage. This was warmly accepted by his adoptive parents.

We continued the process by having James focus holistically on his wellness. Through our discussion he worked at accepting himself physically. He tried to eat healthier and to acknowledge his physical appearance with pride. He worked at developing his emotional well-being by acknowledging his feelings, such as the pain he experienced when his sister called him lazy and the peace he felt when he first honourably believed himself to be a Cree man. His mental well-being was addressed when he recognized that he was able to learn difficult concepts and develop clear insights when he dedicated some attention to these matters. Most importantly, James developed his belief in himself and a sense of purpose. He saw that he had abilities, or as the Elder had stated "gifts," just like everyone else. He was committed to discovering his gifts. This was the beginning of James's spiritual development. It was also his start in trying to discover his personal dreams and aspirations. He was informed that the Elder could assist in this discovery process and was left with the option of connecting with the Elder at his own pace.

James came to recognize that his holistic wellness was intricately tied to his relationship with his biological and adoptive families. He and I spent a significant amount of time developing his understanding of how these relationships are to be nurtured for his and his families' well-being. Importantly, James saw the need to develop a respect for himself as a son in both a Cree and non-Aboriginal family. Respecting both of these aspects of himself, James was better able to develop a more harmonious image of himself in relation to each of his families. While he was not able to connect with his biological family by the time he decided to end the formal time we shared, he developed a degree of comfort of where he stood as a Cree man who was removed from his family of origin. He recognized that this would be an ongoing matter to be reflected upon regularly. He decided to become more involved with the Aboriginal community in the city as he believed that this would allow him to develop a greater appreciation for what his biological parents faced when he was a small child.

James and I ended our time together with a feast in which we honoured the sharing that took place between us. James invited his family once again and I invited the Elder who spent time with the two of us. During this feast, James offered me a small gift of appreciation, which I accepted. He also gave the Elder a blanket as a symbol of his appreciation and tobacco so that he could call for support in the future.

Helping Families

When their work focuses on families, helpers using an Aboriginal approach expand the use of the foundational principles to include the dynamics between family members. Each member of the family is respected and valued by the helper. The acceptance of each family member by all other members is encouraged. In addition, the family as a whole is seen positively, particularly the attributes they hold which can support the members' growth and which contribute to the wellness of the surrounding community. The relationships between members is seen as a focal point for the helping processes. Helpers assist families to review whether these relationships are balanced, in that everyone's contribution to the family is respected by other family members, and to acknowledge and understand the inter-dependence present in the family.

Helpers guide families to consider the harmony of their family and whether the contributions made by family members are supporting their family as a whole as well as each individual in the family. Families are encouraged to determine how they are to achieve centredness together and what it will take for the family to strive towards *mino-pimatisiwin*. In others words, they are encouraged to develop a mutually supportive, if not common-sense of purpose. In order to make these strides, helpers support the family members to reflect upon and share the knowledge of the family history as well as to address issues and concerns which inhibit any member's healing and/or the growth of the family. They are also encouraged, when appropriate, to share their dreams with one another in order to help them to develop their common purpose.

Helpers contribute to the family's awareness that changes to families are normal processes in the cycle of life. Changes, such as the death of a family member, may be beyond the control of the family; at other times, choices made by families, such as moving away from their community of origin, may invoke change. The changes that occur within a family are often influenced by the power structure in the family. Helpers acknowledge the family structure and patterns and direct the family to reflect upon whether they are used for the well-being of all members. Abuses of power are seen as retarding the healing and growth of family members and are discouraged, if not stopped. Family members abusing their power are informed that oppressing others ultimately leads to isolation, individual and family breakdown, and away from *mino-pimatisiwin*. Helpers support the abusive person to recognize that such actions put the wellness of all family members, and indirectly the community, at risk. Indeed, physical abuse is not tolerated and actions are taken to stop it even though this means breaking the ethic of non-interference.

In supporting families, helpers first turn to Elders within a family and seek to establish a particular relationship with them. It is acknowledged that Elders hold much knowledge of the family's history, strengths and challenges and may be able to provide an anchor which defines where the family came from. If other Elders are brought into the helping process, the family Elder has the first opportunity to meet with these people. This is particularly important in smaller communities where the older generations know of one another's histories and abilities. It is also recognized that not all elderly family members are able to take on such a significant role immediately. They themselves may be a source of concern. In such situations, the individual and the individual's experiences are acknowledged and respected, while a focus on the need to address the concerns is clearly maintained.

In addition to incorporating the aid of Elders, helpers use other techniques. For example, they share their own family stories to demonstrate the dynamics in their families, including the challenges their families have faced and how their families overcame these difficulties. In turn, they encourage members to share family stories of success and growth, as well as humourous ones. Helpers also encourage the use of rituals and ceremonies by the family as a whole in order to help them develop their sense of family unity and togetherness. As with work with individuals, when the helping relationship with the family comes to an end, a ceremony, such as a gift exchange or the putting out of candles, marking the end of the cycle and the change in the relationship is completed.

A Case Example with a Family Focus
Wendy Mahikan was a twenty-six-year-old single mother of three children. At the time of our first visit, her oldest child, David, was ten, her younger son, Donny, was six, and her daughter, Christa, was five. Wendy had been living with her parents, Margaret and Moses, in the city when David was born. As Wendy was still quite young at the time, Wendy's parents were very involved in David's upbringing while David's father remained out of the picture. Three years later, Wendy moved out and established her own home with David. She was receiving a bursary to attend university at that time. During her first year academic year, she met Robert at a university social gathering. About a year after they met Wendy was pregnant with Donny. Shortly after the birth of Donny, Wendy became pregnant with Christa. Before Christa was born, Robert graduated, and a year later he left the city to return to his home community in

the north part of the province. He remained in touch with the family by phone and with periodic visits with the children. Soon after Robert left, David began acting out. He began throwing temper tantrums at school and talking back to his mom. Usually these incidents were followed by David apologizing and crying for acting in such a manner. Despite the apologies, these dynamics continued and escalated to the point where David threatened to hit his mom.

In addition, Wendy's father passed away last year from complications related to diabetes. Her mother has been relying on Wendy for support ever since and stays at Wendy's three-bedroom townhouse apartment most nights. This created further stress on Wendy who became resentful of her mother's presence. Wendy was also feeling overwhelmed with meeting all the demands placed upon her. She started drinking on weekends, which affected her studies. Early one Friday evening, a Child and Family Services worker came to Wendy's home to find Wendy passed out drunk while the kids were playing. A few minutes later, Wendy's mother arrived to spend the night and was able to convince the worker that everything would be all right as she would be taking care of the matter. The worker stated that she would be following up on the situation with Wendy and left. Wendy called our office for services on the following Monday after she and her mother had an argument about the incident. She stated that she had reached her limit and had to turn things around. She believed that she couldn't make such changes on her own and wanted someone to talk with her and her family.

In working with the Mahikan family, I ensured that I acknowledged Wendy's mother as soon as possible. I was careful not to present myself as aligning with Margaret, or any other family member for that matter, but I wanted to demonstrate respect to Margaret as the eldest of the family. In the initial meeting with the family, I sought to develop a relationship with each family member and to demonstrate that I would listen to each of their views. The initial meeting focused on gaining a picture of the presenting concern. I noted it was difficult for Wendy to hear her mother's views on Wendy's parenting and for David to hear about his actions from either his mother or grandmother. Indeed, each family member would attempt to cut in and give their view of the situation discussed. To offset this process, we agreed to use a sharing circle in this session so that each person would have the opportunity to present their understanding without interruption from others. For the most part, the circle was completed with everyone giving each other a chance to speak their mind. The exceptions were Christa, who was too young, and Donny, who shyly remained quiet. This circle was beneficial for the family since each member was able to be heard by other family members. This provided the opportunity to discuss the need for balance within the family, particularly in relation to how they were going to support one another. In a following session, each family member was able to define how they could contribute to the well-being of the family. Significant to this part of the process was the opportunity for Wendy to accept support from her mother without feeling like she was a teenager struggling to gain her voice in the raising of her children. Margaret was able to relay family stories of struggle with similar inter-generational issues. In this way she was able to establish a new connection with Wendy.

As the helper, I introduced the concept of harmony and had the family consider what the family would be like if they were working together harmoniously. This provided each family member the opportunity to consider how their behaviour supported or interfered with the family's well-being. Wendy spoke of how her need to be seen as independent was interfering with her need to accept support from other family members. She also spoke of how her refusal of support from her mother was interfering with the family's ability to address David's needs. Margaret was then able to offer support to Wendy by spending time with David. This gave Wendy time she desired for her studies. It also gave David time to reconnect with his grandmother and grieve over the loses of his stepfather and grandfather. This was significant because the reconnection helped David overcome the feelings of loss associated with his emotional separation from his grandfather. It also helped Margaret move through her own grief.

Another concept introduced was *mino-pimatisiwin*. Each family member was asked to describe what a good life would mean to them individually and to the family. By first describing their thoughts individually, the family was able to establish a common family goal. This included remembering the family members who have passed on through an annual feast in which they would recall stories of those family members and eat food that reminded them of the whole family. It was apparent that such a ceremony would also serve to bring the family closer together. Another goal was supporting Wendy in finishing her studies. They recognized that this would require all members to chip in by completing daily, age appropriate tasks. This provided Wendy the time she needed and provided Margaret with a sense of purpose and contribution. Later, the family discovered that this also helped David to see his behaviour in relation to his family.

Throughout these few meetings with the family, my role as a helper was limited. I served as someone who got them to consider themselves in relation to the family as a whole. This often involved asking questions which were applied to all family members and encouraging them to reflect on their ideas in relation to each other. These questions were framed within the foundational concepts of holism, connections and relationships, balance, harmony and *mino-pimatisiwin*. Obviously, this process was influenced by the age and abilities of the children, but when appropriate and as much as possible, the children were given the opportunity to voice their thoughts and express their feelings.

While there were outstanding issues which remained, such as Wendy's grief over the death of her father, the role of spirituality in the family's grieving process, the balance between meeting parental obligations and academic requirements, and the patterns that were being passed on intergenerationally, the family chose to end the meetings for the time being. The general consensus was that they wanted time to implement the ideas they had discussed. I respected the family's need to go at their own pace and expressed my openness to seeing them in the future. The last session ended with sharing of snack crackers and juice, as suggested by David and Christa, and a closing sharing circle in which I expressed my sincere appreciation for being allowed to receive the gift of their family story.

Helping Groups

The Aboriginal approach can be used with non-familial groups, with helpers using the foundational concepts as a guide for the group processes. Such groups can include those orientated to self development, addressing experiences of childhood abuse and supporting couples in re-strengthening their relationships. These groups may even elect to use a sharing circle format, thus incorporating an Aboriginal approach overtly and directly. To initiate the "birth" of the group, helpers incorporate a ceremony, such as opening songs and/or a feast to mark its beginning. As a group moves through whichever process it follows, helpers ensure that the group members are respectful of one another. Respect is explained in terms of listening, patience, waiting for people to finish speaking and remaining open to hearing from others. Helpers acknowledge that while they are facilitators for groups, they are only one source of help within groups. They openly encourage people to share their life experiences with one another, since all members are valued as carriers of knowledge which can help other people and as teachers who can offer guidance. Group members are encouraged to speak from their hearts.

Helpers following an Aboriginal approach walk groups through processes which assist them to establish their own goals. As well, individuals within the group are supported to establish goals which contribute to their own well-being and the well-being of the group. Helpers outline the meaning of *mino-pimatisiwin* and the other foundational concepts, which then guide the group as it works towards its goals. For example, if one person or a few people dominate the sharing, helpers remind the group of the concept of balance and encourage all group members to share their ideas. Thus, while not forcing people to speak, they open the opportunity for others to share and directly and/or indirectly remind the dominating members of the values of respect. People who demonstrate a significant amount of power within the group are encouraged to use this power to support each group member and the group as a whole. They are also encouraged to accept the other members' explanation of how this support is to be offered. As another example, helpers encourage all group participants to reflect upon the relationships they have established with other group members. Such reflection would include how they made the connections, how they may be avoiding such connections, and how their part in the relationship is contributing to the wellness of themselves and each group member. During the life of the group, helpers encourage participants to remember that humility, not judgement, is to be exercised. This is one way in which helpers maintain a sense of balance between the needs and well-being of individuals and the group as a whole.

Helpers may elicit the guidance of Elders, who may be brought into the group regularly or for a specific number of sessions to address specific tasks. Helpers ensure that the contributing Elders are given time to share their experiences and knowledge of the matters being addressed by the group and group members. Elders may conduct rituals, such as smudging or pipe ceremonies, as part of the group process. They may act as support to the group by being available for additional guidance and/or ceremonies outside the regular group meetings. As with the start of the group, helpers incorporate a ceremony to mark the completion of a group's cycle. Such closings may involve a sharing circle focused on the closing of the group processes, songs and/or a feast. The ceremony acknowledges the changes that have occurred and the changes in the relationships of the group members with the ending of the group. Finally, helpers recognize that while their relationships with group members is changing, it may continue with different parameters. Thus, they remain open to the people.

Addressing Specific Issues: Family Violence

The Aboriginal approach can guide helpers to address specific issues. Violence is an abuse of power that greatly limits, if not stops, all family members' abilities to seek and reach *mino-pimatisiwin*. When working to address the issue of family violence, helpers recognize that violence directly affects people holistically. People are affected emotionally, through living in a state of constant fear, and the physical effects include bruising or a change in eating patterns. Helpers also recognize spiritual effects such as the disconnection from life essence and the degraded sense of self that often results for the abused and the abuser. Mental effects, including the rationalization of the abuse and inability to consider alternative options, are also acknowledged. Helpers also see the influence each of these effects has on the others. For example, a constant nervous tension can cause a sick feeling in one's stomach, which leads to increases/decreases in eating. Family violence destroys the harmony of the family by allowing little, if any, peace within and between members. Members are unable to respect one another or share any positive strength that could help move them out of the destructive cycle. Instead, the family's focus remains on the upcoming abuse. Members are unable to fully reflect on their own lives and in turn are unable to develop a strong sense of individual centredness or to support the family's sense of centredness. Families and individuals within families are faced with barriers that limit, even stop, their healing and growth.

In attempting to change these processes, the first concern of helpers following an Aboriginal approach is to address those actions, particularly the abuse, which stop or hinder learning, healing and growth. Like the fluxes found throughout the universe that overcome and change patterns and cycles, stopping the abuse will likely require breaking the ethic of non-interference in order to ensure each family member's safety. For example, helpers may provide support to the abused person in moving or in having the police remove the offender. Helpers work to establish a strong relationship with the family as a whole and with each individual. This is accomplished through maintaining the values of respect and sharing. For example, helpers listen to the stories and experiences of family members and share their experiences with and knowledge of such events. This does not mean that violence is accepted, but it is seen as an unacceptable action perpetrated by individuals who have the ability to change their behaviour. Helpers teach family members about the history behind such oppressive acts and seek to learn of the family's history as understood by each family member.

Once the family has offered its acceptance and trust, the helper supports each family member to explore how the violence has affected them emotionally, physically, mentally and spiritually. This self-awareness is built upon by the helper and individuals in exploring ways to heal the hurt and destruction in each area. This may include such actions as supporting the expression of repressed feelings, encouraging a proper diet and physical activity, teaching about alternative ways to deal with issues affecting the family and supporting the re-establishment of spiritual connections within themselves and with others through participation in ceremonies, services and meditation. Family members and the family as a whole are supported to develop goals related to overcoming the effects of the violence. To prepare them in developing these goals, they are informed of *mino-pimatisiwin* and how violence leads people away from it. They are also reminded and/or taught about the role of dreams and visions and are encouraged to incorporate their dreams and visions as part of their goals.

To help family members to change the patterns of abuse, Elders with an understanding of how violence leads people away from *mino-pimatisiwin* are sought out as supports for the family. Family members are reminded that, while they are not responsible for the abuse, they are responsible for their own healing and growth. Thus, each member is supported to develop a greater understanding of themselves and encouraged to support other members in their healing and growth processes. Families are informed of how ceremonies can support them to establish new patterns and connections with one another and within. They are encouraged to incorporate personal and family ceremonies within these new patterns. They are reminded about the positive aspects of life. They are then supported to find these aspects in the events that they have endured and to use them in reaching their goals.

While this process may have been brought on by a sudden change, such as the removal of the offending family member, it is recognized by helpers that new patterns take time to establish. They are prepared to walk with the family as much and as long as possible. They also recognize the restraints placed upon them and the families, such as the influences of those who want the original pattern to stay the same. Such individuals may try to undermine efforts of the helper by not participating, by calling down the helper or by threatening family members further. These restraints are acknowledged and the family is informed of them. Helpers following an Aboriginal approach accept that their relationships with families overcoming abuse are likely to be long-lasting once established. When the time comes that the helper is not able to continue to offer assistance in the same manner, a ceremony is held to support the family and the helper in the transition process.

Through the entire process, helpers are active in seeking their own balance, connectedness, harmony and centredness. When a helper is overcome by the issues raised by the family, it is acknowledged honestly and openly by themselves. Helpers facing such a situation take responsibility to re-establish themselves for the well-being of themselves and the families they are working with. They remain willing to share how they are doing this, since they are acting as role models and legitimizing the intensity of the issues for all those involved. They also ensure that they do not hinder the family's own healing process with the helper's own issues. In other words, while there is openness to the helper's healing, the helper ensures such openness does not interfere with the family's focus on their own healing.

Addressing Specific Issues: Self-Esteem in Youth

When using an Aboriginal approach to help groups of individuals, sharing circles can be incorporated, for example, in fostering the self-esteem development of youth. The circle of courage (Brendtro, Brokenleg and Van Bockern 1998), for example, is based on establishing in youth the four spirits of belonging, mastery, independence and generosity. Such groups consist of a facilitator familiar with the circle of courage, an Elder and up to twelve youth who meet for a total of six occasions. The first meeting focuses on helping all participants to establish respectful relationships with one another, and utilizes four rounds of sharing using circle processes. The first round begins with an opening prayer and ceremony, such as a pipe ceremony, the facilitator and Elder introducing themselves, and then the youths introducing themselves. In the second round the facilitator outlines the purpose of the group and agenda for each meeting, and each youth is given the opportunity to share on these matters. The Elder finishes the second round. The third round begins with the facilitator outlining the guidelines for the sharing circles, including an explanation of the foundational concepts and values, and then requesting that the youth participate in establishing the ground rules for the group. Each youth is given the opportunity to comment on the guidelines and express suggestions for the ground rules. The Elder then shares traditional ways in which groups functioned and the rules they followed. Finally, there is a check-out round where each person is given the opportunity to share their feelings and thoughts prior to the closing prayer.

The second meeting addresses belonging. The Elder begins with an opening prayer and initiates the check-in round by outlining the need for us to be aware of ourselves emotionally, physically, mentally and spiritually. Each youth then checks in followed by the facilitator. The facilitator begins the second round by explaining the importance of belonging to a person's self-esteem and outlining distorted and absent ways of belonging. The youth are then given the opportunity to speak about their spirit of belongingness with their family, friends and community and how its presence or absence has affected them emotionally, physically, mentally and spiritually. The round closes with the Elder outlining traditional ways in which Aboriginal people supported belongingness and what happens when it is absent. The third round begins with the facilitator outlining normal ways of establishing the spirit of belonging, followed by each youth being given the opportunity to speak on how they could better support their own spirit of belonging. The round ends with the Elder sharing experiential stories which support the spirit of belonging. The final round is a check-out round and is completed with a closing prayer by the Elder.

The third meeting focuses the spirit of mastery and follows the same format of four sharing circles: check-in, an explanation of mastery and distorted expressions of it, healthy ways of showing one's spirit of mastery and check-out. In the same manner, the fourth and fifth meetings focus on the spirit of independence and the spirit of generosity respectively. The final meeting begins with an opening prayer and a check-in round. The second round has the participants sharing what they are taking with them as a result of the meetings. The facilitator also summarizes the process the youth have gone through and gives an overview of the foundational concepts and values they demonstrated in the sharing circles. The third round includes a ceremony, such as a pipe ceremony, and closing comments by the Elder. The final round consists of each participant acknowledging each other participant.

By the end of all the meetings, the youth will have experienced six sharing circles with twenty-four rounds of sharing. They will have seen the process modelled by the facilitator and Elder and will have incorporated the foundational concepts and values through their participation. The focus on self-esteem will have been maintained and the entire experience will have reaffirmed Aboriginal worldviews and practices.

NOTES

1. While all of the case examples within this chapter are based upon my helping experiences with various individuals and families, they are fictitious.

REFERENCES

Absolon, K. 1993. *Healing as Practice: Teachings from the Medicine Wheel.* A commissioned paper for the WUNSKA network, Canadian Schools of Social Work. Unpublished manuscript.

Aitken, L.P. 1990. The cultural basis for Indian medicine. In L.P. Aitken and E.W. Haller.

Aitken, L.P., and E.W. Haller (eds.). 1990. *Two Cultures Meet: Pathways for American Indians to Medicine.* Garrett Park, MD: Garrett Park Press.

Anderson, K. 2000. *A Recognition of Being: Reconstructing Native Womanhood.* Toronto: Second Story Press.

Antone, B., and D. Hill. 1990. *Traditional Healing: Helping Our People Lift Their Burdens.* London, ON: Tribal Sovereign Associates.

Asikinack, W. 1995. "Anishinabe (Ojibway) legends through Anishinabe eyes." In O.P. Dickason.

Assembly of First Nations. 1994. *Breaking the Silence.* Ottawa, ON: First Nations Health Commission.

Attneave, C. 1982. "American Indians and Alaska Native families: Emigrants in their own homeland." In M. McGoldrick, J.K. Pearce, and J. Giordano.

Auger, R. 1994. "Rose Auger: Buffalo Robe Medicine Lodge." In S. Johnston.

Baker, Chief S., and V.J. Kirkness. 1994. *Khot-la-cha: The Autobiography of Chief Simon Baker.* Vancouver, BC: Douglas and McIntyre.

Barman, J., Y. Hebert and D. McCaskill (eds.). 1987. *Indian Education in Canada: Volume 2: The Challenge.* Vancouver, BC: University of British Columbia Press.

Battiste, M., and J. Barman (eds.). 1995. *First Nations Education in Canada: The Circle Unfolds.* Vancouver, BC: UBC Press.

Battiste, M., and J.S.Y. Henderson. 2000. *Protecting Indigenous Knowledge and Heritage: A Global Challenge.* Saskatoon, SK: Purich Publishing.

Benton-Banai, E. 1988. *The Mishomis Book.* Saint Paul, MN: Red School House.

Boldt, M., and J.A. Long. 1984. "Tribal traditions and European-Western political ideologies: The dilemma of Canada's Native Indians." *Canadian Journal of Political Science XVII,* 3: 537–53.

Bopp, J., M. Bopp, L. Brown, and P. Lane. 1985. *The Sacred Tree* (2nd ed.). Lethbridge, AB: Four Worlds Development Press.

Brendtro, L., M. Brokenleg. and S. Van Bockern. 1998. *Reclaiming Youth at Risk: Our Hope for the Future.* Bloomington, IN: National Education Service.

Brant, C. 1990. "Native ethics and rules of behaviour." *Canadian Journal of Psychiatry* 35: 534–39.

Briks, M. 1983. "I have the power within to heal myself and to find truth." Tumak's cousin (fifty-five minutes with a Native Elder). *The Social Woker/Le Travailleur Social* 51, 2: 47–48.

Broken Nose, M.A. 1992. "Working with the Oglala Lakota: An outsider's perspective." *Families in Society: The Journal of Contemporary Human Services* 73, 6: 380–84.

Bruchac, J. 1992. "Storytelling and the sacred: On the use of Native American stories." In B. Slapin and D. Seale.

Bucko, R.A. 1998. *The Lakota Ritual of the Sweat Lodge: History and Contemporary Practice*. Lincoln: University of Nebraska Press.

Burgest, D.R. (ed.). 1989. *Social Work Practice with Minorities* (2nd ed.). Metuchen, NJ: Scarecrow Press.

Cajete, G. 1999. *Igniting the Sparkle: An Indigenous Science Education Model*. Skyand, NC: Kivaki Press.

_____. 1994. *Look to the Mountain: An Ecology of Indigenous Education*. Durango, CO: Kivaki Press.

Calliou, S. 1995. "Peacekeeping actions at home: A medicine wheel model for a peacekeeping pedagogy." In M. Battiste and J. Barman.

Canadian Association of Social Workers. 1994. "The social work profession and the Aboriginal peoples: CASW presentation to the Royal Commission on Aboriginal peoples." *The Social Worker* 62,4: 158.

Canadian Plains Research Centre. 1979. *The Proceedings of the Plains Cree Conference*. Regina, SK: Canadian Plains Research Centre, University of Regina.

Canda, E.R. 1983. "General implications of shamanism for clinical social work." *International Social Work* XXVI, 4: 14–22.

Clarkson, L., V. Morrissette and G. Regallet. 1992. *Our Responsibility to the Seventh Generation: Indigenous Peoples and Sustainable Development*. Winnipeg, MB: International Institute for Sustainable Development.

Coggins, K. 1990. *Alternative Pathways to Healing: The Recovery Medicine Wheel*. Deerfield Beach, FL: Health Communications.

Compton, B. R., and Galaway, B. 1994. *Social Work Processes* (5th ed.). Pacific Grove, CA: Brooks/Cole Publishing Company.

Couture, J.E. 1996. "The role of Native Elders: Emergent issues." In D.A. Long and O.P. Dickason.

Deloria, V. Jr. 1999. *For This Land: Writings on Religion in America*. New York: Routledge.

Dickason, O.P. (ed.). 1995. *The Native Imprint: The Contribution of First Peoples to Canada's Character, Volume 1: to 1815*. Athabasca, AB: Athabasca University Educational Enterprises.

Dion Buffalo, Y.R. 1990. "Seeds of thought, arrows of change: Native storytelling as metaphor." In T.A. Laidlaw, C. Malmo and Associates.

Dugan, K.M. 1985. *The Vision Quest of the Plains Indians: Its Spiritual Significance*. Lewiston, NY: The Edwin Mellen Press.

Duran, E., and B. Duran. 1995. *Native American Postcolonial Psychology*. Albany, NY: State University of New York Press.

Dusenberry, V. 1962. *The Montana Cree: A Study in Religious Persistence*. Stockholm, Sweden: Almquist and Wiksell.

Ellison Williams, E., and F. Ellison. 1996. Culturally informed social work practice with American Indian clients: Guidelines for non-Indian social workers. *Social Work* 41, 2: 14–151.

Englestad, D., and J. Bird (eds.). 1992. *Nation to Nation: Aboriginal Sovereignty and the Future of Canada.* Concord, ON: Anansi Press.

Ermine, W. 1995. "Aboriginal epistemology." In M. Battiste and J. Barman.

Ferrara, N. 1999. *Emotional Expression Among Cree Indians: The Role of Pictorial Representations in the Assessment of Psychological Mindedness.* Philadelphia, PA: Jessica Kingsley Publishers.

Fournier, S., and E. Crey. 1997. *Stolen From Our Embrace.* Vancouver, BC: Douglas and McIntyre.

Freire, P. 1993. *Pedagogy of the Oppressed* (new revised 20th anniversary ed.). New York: Continuum.

Gaywish, R. 2000. "Aboriginal People and Mainstream Dispute Resolution: Cultural Implications of Use." In J. Oakes, R. Riewe, S. Koolage, L. Simpson and N. Schuster.

Gil, D.G. 1998. *Confronting Injustice and Oppression: Concepts and Strategies for Social Workers.* New York: Columbia University Press.

Good Tracks, J.G. 1989. "Native American noninterference." In D.R. Burgest.

Guay, S. 1994. *Peer Counselling.* Ottawa, ON: National Association of Friendship Centres.

"Guidelines for Talking Circles." 1990. *The Four World Exchange* 1, 4: 11–12.

Hallowell, A.I. 1992. *The Ojibwa of Berens River, Manitoba: Ethnography in History.* Toronto, ON: Harcourt Brace Ivanovich College Publishers.

Hamilton, A.C., and C.M. Sinclair. 1991. *Volume 1: Report of the Aboriginal Justice Inquiry of Manitoba.* Winnipeg, MB: Queen's Printer.

Hampton, M., E. Hampton, G. Kinunwa and L. Kinunwa. 1995. "Alaska recovery and spirit camps: First Nations community development." *Community Development Journal* 30, 3: 257–64.

Hart, M.A. 1996. "Sharing circles: Utilizing traditional practice methods for teaching, helping, and supporting." In O'Meara and West.

Herring, R.D. 1996. "Synergetic counseling and Native American Indian students." *Journal of Counseling and Development* 74, 6: 542–47.

Hodgson, M. 1992. "Rebuilding community after the residential school experience." In D. Englestad and J. Bird.

Hollow Water Community Holistic Circle Healing. 1993. *Position on Incarceration.* Unpublished manuscript.

Irwin, L. 1994. "Dreams, Theory, and Culture: The Plains Vision Quest Paradigm." *American Indian Quarterly* 18, 2: 229–45.

Janzen, H.L., S. Skakum and W. Lightning. 1994. "Professional services in a Cree Native community." *Canadian Journal of School Psychology* 10, 1: 88–102.

Johnson, P. 1983. *Native Children and the Child Welfare System.* Toronto, ON: Canadian Council on Social Development in association with James Lorimer and Company.

Johnston, B. 1976. *Ojibway Heritage.* Toronto, ON: McClelland and Stewart.

Johnston, S. (ed.). 1994. *The Book of Elders: The Life Stories and Wisdom of Great American Indians.* New York: Harper Collins.

Katz, R., and V. St. Denis. 1991. "Teachers as healers." *Journal of Indigenous Studies* 2, 2: 23–36.

LaDue, R.A. 1994. "Coyote returns: Twenty sweats does not an Indian expert make." *Women and Therapy* 15, 1: 93–111.

Laidlaw, T.A., C. Malmo and Associates. 1990. *Healing Voices: Feminist Approaches to Therapy With Women.* San Francisco, CA: Jossey-Bass Publishers.

Levitt, K.L., and B. Wharf (eds.). 1985. *Challenge of Child Wlefare.* Vancouver: University of British Columbia Press.

"Listening to the Elders: 2." 1992. *The Four Worlds Exchange* 2, 3: 20–21.

Little Bear, L. 1998. "Aboriginal relationships to the land and resources." In J. Oakes, R. Riewe, K. Kinew and E. Maloney.

Long, D.A., and O.P. Dickason. 1996. *Visions of the Heart: Canadian Aboriginal Issues.* Toronto, ON: Harcourt Brace and Company.

Long, D.A. and T. Fox. 1996. "Circles of healing: Illness, Healing, and Health among Aboriginal people in Canada." In D.A. Long and O.P. Dickason.

Longclaws, L.N. 1994. "Social work and the medicine wheel framework." In B.R. Compton and B. Galaway.

Longclaws, L.N., P. Rosebush, and L.J. Barkwell. 1993. *Report of the Wawayseecappo First Nation Domestic Violence Project.* Submitted to Solicitor General of Canada, Corrections Branch, Ministry Secretariat, Contract no. 1514-93/wa1-525.

Malloch, L. 1989. "Indian medicine, Indian health: Study between red and white medicine." *Canadian Women Studies* 10, 2/3: 105–12.

Mawhiney, A.M. (ed.). 1993. *Rebirth: Political, Economic, and Social Development in First Nations.* Toronto, ON: Dundurn Press.

_____. 1995. "The First Nations in Canada." In J.C. Turner and F.J. Turner.

McCormick, R. 1995. "The facilitation of healing for the First Nations people of British Columbia." *Canadian Journal of Native Education* 21, 2: 251–322.

McGoldrick, M. J.K. Pearce and J. Giordano. 1982. *Ethnicity and Family Therapy.* New York: Guilford Press.

McKenzie, B. 1985. "Social work practice with Natives." In S. Yelaja.

McKenzie, B., and B. Hudson. 1985. "Native children, child welfare and the colonization of Native people." In K. L. Levitt and B. Wharf.

McKenzie, B., and L. Morrissette. 1993. "Cultural empowerment and healing." In A.M. Mawhiney.

McPherson, D.H., and J.D. Rabb. 1993. *Indians from the inside: A study in ethno-metaphysics.* Thunder Bay, ON: Centre for Northern Studies, Lakehead University.

Medicine, B. 1987. "My Elders tell me." In J. Barman, Y. Hebert and D. McCaskill.

Meili, D. 1991. *Those Who Know: Profiles of Alberta's Native Elders.* Edmonton,

ON: NeWest Publishers.

Memmi, A. 1991. *The Colonized and the Colonizer.* Boston, MA: Beacon Press.

Morrisseau, C. 1998. *Into the Daylight: A Wholistic Approach to Healing.* Toronto, ON: University of Toronto Press.

Morrissette, V., B. McKenzie and L. Morrissette. 1993. "Towards an Aboriginal model of social work practice: Cultural knowledge and traditional practices." *Canadian Social Work Review* 10, 1: 91–108.

Nabigon, H. (nd.). *The Hollow Tree.* Unpublished manuscript.

_____. 1993. "Reclaiming the spirit for First Nations government." In A.M. Mawhiney.

Nelson, C.H., M.L. Kelley and D.H. McPherson. 1985. "Rediscovering support in social work practice: Lessons from Indian Indigenous human service workers." *Canadian Social Work Review* 2, 231–48.

Niezen, R. 1993. "Telling a message: Cree perceptions of custom and administration." *The Canadian Journal of Native Studies* XIII, 2: 221–50.

Oakes, J., R. Riewe, K. Kinew and E. Maloney (eds.). 1998. *Sacred Lands: Aboriginal World Views, Claims, and Conflicts.* Edmonton: Canadian Circumpolar Institute, University of Alberta and Department of Native Studies, University of Manitoba.

Oakes, J., R. Riewe, S. Koolage, L. Simpson and N. Schuster (eds.). 2000. *Aboriginal Health, Identity and Resources.* Winnipeg, MB: Departments of Native Studies and Zoology, and Faculty of Graduates Studies, University of Manitoba.

Odjig White, L. 1996. "Medicine wheel teaching in Native language education." In S. O'Meara and D.A. West.

O'Meara, S. 1996. "Epilogue." In S. O'Meara and D.A. West.

O'Meara, S., and D.A. West (eds.). 1996. *From Our Eyes: Learning from Indigenous Peoples.* Toronto, ON: Garamond Press.

Overholt, T.W., and J.B. Callicott. 1982. *Clothed in fur and other tails: An introduction to an Ojibwa world view.* Washington, DC: University Press of America.

Peat, F.D. 1994. *Lighting the Seventh Fire: The Spiritual Ways, Healing, and Science of the Native American.* Toronto, ON: Canadian Manda Group.

Pepper, F.C., and S.L. Henry. 1991. "An Indian perspective of self-esteem." *Canadian Journal of Native Education* 18, 2: 145–60.

Poproski, D.L. 1997. "Healing experiences of British Columbia First Nations women: Moving beyond suicide ideation and intention." *Canadian Journal of Community Mental Health* 16, 2: 69–90.

Red Horse, J.G. 1980. "American Indian Elders: Unifiers of Indian Families." *Social Casework* 61, 8.

Regnier, R. 1994. "The sacred circle: A process pedagogy of healing." *Interchange* 25,2: 129–44.

_____. 1995. "The sacred circle: An Aboriginal approach to healing education at an urban high school." In M. Battiste and J Barman.

Ridington, R. 1982. "Telling secrets: Stories of the vision quest." *The Canadian Journal of Native Studies* II, 2: 213–19.

Ross, R. 1996. *Returning to the Teachings*. Toronto. ON: Penguin Books.

Royal Commission on Aboriginal Peoples. 1997. *Report of the Royal Commission on Aboriginal Peoples*. Ottawa. ON: Minister of Supply and Services Canada.

Schwager, K.W., A.M. Mawhiney and J. Lewko. 1991. "Cultural aspects of prevention programs." *Canadian Social Work Review* 8, 2: 246–54

Scott, K.J. 1991. "Alice Modig and the talking circle." *The Canadian Nurse* June: 25–26.

Slapin, B., and D. Seale (eds.). *1992. Through Indian Eyes: The Native Experience in Books for Children*. Gabriola Island, BC: New Society Publishers.

Smith, L.T. 1999. "Colonizing knowledges." In *Decolonizing Methodologies: Research and Indigenous Peoples*. London, UK: Zed Books.

Stevenson, J. 1999. "The circle of healing." *Native Social Work Journal: Nishnaabe Kinoomaadwin Naadmaadwin* 2, 1: 91–112.

Stiegelbauer, S.M. 1996. "What is an Elder? What do Elders do?: First Nations Elders as teachers in culture-based urban organizations." *The Canadian Journal of Native Studies* XVI, 1: 37–66.

Tofoya, T. 1989. "Circles and cedar: Native Americans and family therapy." *Journal of Psychotherapy and the Family* 6: 71–98.

Turner, J.C., and F.J. Turner (eds.). 1995. *Canadian Social Welfare* (3rd ed.) Scarborough, ON: Allyn and Bacon Canada.

Vandenbroek, B. 1998. "Sacred lands: Living in harmony." In J. Oakes, R. Riewe, K. Kinew and E. Maloney.

Waldram, J.B. 1994. "Aboriginal spirituality in corrections: A Canadian case study in religion and therapy." *American Indian Quarterly* 18, 2: 197–214.

_____. 1997. *The Way of the Pipe*. Peterborough, On: Broadview Press.

Wilkinson, G.T. 1980. "On assisting Indian people." *Social Casework* 61, 8: 451–52.

Yelaja, S. 1985. *An Introduction to Social Work Practice in Canada*. Scarborough, ON: Prentice-Hall.

Young, D., G. Ingram and L. Swartz. 1989. *Cry of the Eagle: Encounters with a Cree Healer*. Toronto, ON: University of Toronto Press.

Young, W. 1999. "Aboriginal students speak about acceptance, sharing, awareness and support: A participatory approach to change at a university and community college." *Native Social Work Journal* 2, 1: 21–58.

Zieba, R.A. 1990. *Healing and Healers Among the Northern Cree*. Unpublished master's thesis, University of Manitoba, Winnipeg, Manitoba.